OECD Reviews of Tertiary Education

Netherlands

Simon Marginson, Thomas Weko, Nicola Channon,
Terttu Luukkonen and Jon Oberg

ORGANISATION FOR ECONOMIC CO-OPERATION AND DEVELOPMENT

The OECD is a unique forum where the governments of 30 democracies work together to address the economic, social and environmental challenges of globalisation. The OECD is also at the forefront of efforts to understand and to help governments respond to new developments and concerns, such as corporate governance, the information economy and the challenges of an ageing population. The Organisation provides a setting where governments can compare policy experiences, seek answers to common problems, identify good practice and work to co-ordinate domestic and international policies.

The OECD member countries are: Australia, Austria, Belgium, Canada, the Czech Republic, Denmark, Finland, France, Germany, Greece, Hungary, Iceland, Ireland, Italy, Japan, Korea, Luxembourg, Mexico, the Netherlands, New Zealand, Norway, Poland, Portugal, the Slovak Republic, Spain, Sweden, Switzerland, Turkey, the United Kingdom and the United States. The Commission of the European Communities takes part in the work of the OECD.

OECD Publishing disseminates widely the results of the Organisation's statistics gathering and research on economic, social and environmental issues, as well as the conventions, guidelines and standards agreed by its members.

This work is published on the responsibility of the Secretary-General of the OECD. The opinions expressed and arguments employed herein do not necessarily reflect the official views of the Organisation or of the governments of its member countries.

Corrigenda to OECD publications may be found on line at: *www.oecd.org/publishing/corrigenda*.

© OECD 2008

Table of contents

This report is based on a study visit to the Netherlands in April-May 2006, and on background documents prepared to support the visit. As a result, the report reflects the situation up to that point.

Glossary

AWT	Advisory Council for Science and Technology
CPB	Netherlands Bureau for Economic Policy Analysis
EFQM	European Foundation for Quality Management
HAVO	The HAVO (*Hoger Algemeen Voortgezet Onderwijs*, literally, "higher general continuing education") has five grades and is attended from age twelve to seventeen. A HAVO diploma provides access to the HBO level of tertiary education.
HBO	*Hoger Beroeps Onderwijs*, a higher professional education
HBO-Raad	HBO Council, the central body representing HBO institutions
Hogescholen	Tertiary institutions providing higher professional education
HOOP	Higher Education and Research Plan (*Hoger Onderwijs en Onderzoek Plan*)
KNAW	Netherlands Royal Academy of Sciences (*Koninklijke Nederlandse Akademie van Wetenschappen*)
LNV	Ministry of Agriculture, Nature and Food Quality
MBO	MBO (*Middelbaar Beroeps Onderwijs*, literally, "middle-level vocational education") is oriented towards vocational training. Many pupils with a VMBO-diploma attend MBO. MBO lasts three to four years. After MBO, pupils can enroll in HBO or enter the job market.
NWO	The Netherlands Organisation for Scientific Research
NOWT	Netherlands Observatory on Science and Technology
NVAO	Netherlands-Flanders Accreditation Organisation
OCW	Ministry of Education, Culture and Science

SME	Small and medium-sized employers
VMBO	The VMBO (*Voorbereidend Middelbaar Beroepsonderwijs*, literally, "preparatory middle-level vocational education") education lasts four years, typically from age twelve to sixteen. It combines vocational training with theoretical education in languages, mathematics, history, arts, and sciences. Sixty percent of students nationally are enrolled in VMBO. VMBO itself has four different levels, in each a different mix of practical vocational training and theoretical education is combined.
VNO-NCW	Dutch employer association for large enterprises
VSNU	Association of Netherlands Research Universities
VWO	VWO (*Voorbereidend Wetenschappelijk Onderwijs*, literally, "preparatory scientific education"). A six year course of theoretical/academic education, typically from age 12 to 18. A VWO diploma provides access to WO training, although certain profiles (combinations of subjects) are required for admittance to study certain subjects.
WO	*Wetenschappelijk Onderwijs*, (literally "scientific education") theoretical/academic education provided at a research university

1. Introduction

1.1 Purposes of the OECD Review

This Country Note on the Netherlands forms part of the OECD Thematic Review of Tertiary Education. This is a collaborative project to assist countries in the design and implementation of tertiary education policies that contribute to the realisation of their social and economic objectives.

The tertiary education systems of many OECD countries have experienced rapid growth over the last decade, and are experiencing new pressures as the result of a globalising economy and labour market. In this context, the OECD Education Committee agreed, in late 2003, to carry out a major thematic review of tertiary education. The principal objective of the review is to assist countries in understanding how the organisation, management and delivery of tertiary education can help them to achieve their economic and social objectives. The principal focus of the review is upon tertiary education policies and systems, rather than upon the detailed management and operation of institutions.

The project's purposes, methodology and guidelines are detailed in OECD (2004a).[1] The purposes of the review are:

- To synthesise research-based evidence on the impact of tertiary education policies and disseminate this knowledge among participating countries;

- To identify innovative and successful policy initiatives and practices;

- To facilitate exchanges of lessons and experiences among countries; and

- To identify policy options.

---

[1] Reports and updates are available from www.oecd.org/edu/tertiary/review

The review encompasses the full range of tertiary programmes and institutions. International statistical conventions define tertiary education in terms of programme levels: those programmes at ISCED[2] levels 5B, 5A and 6 are treated as tertiary education, and programmes below ISCED level 5B are not. In some countries the term higher education is used more commonly than tertiary education, at times to refer to all programmes at levels 5B, 5A and 6, at times to refer only to those programmes at levels 5A and 6. An additional complication is presented by the practice, in some countries, of defining higher education or tertiary education in terms of the institution, rather than the programme. For example, it is common to use higher education to refer to programmes offered by universities, and tertiary education to refer to programmes offered by institutions that extend beyond universities. The OECD thematic review follows standard international conventions in using tertiary education to refer to all programmes at ISCED levels 5B, 5A and 6, regardless of the institutions in which they are offered.

The project involves two complementary approaches: an *Analytical Review strand;* and a *Country Review strand.* The Analytical Review strand uses several means – country background reports, literature reviews, data analyses and commissioned papers – to analyse the factors that shape the outcomes in tertiary education systems, and possible policy responses. All of the 24 countries involved in the Review are taking part in this strand. In addition, 13 of the tertiary education systems have chosen to participate in a Country Review, which involves external review teams analysing tertiary education policies in those countries.

The Netherlands was one of the countries that opted to participate in the Country Reviews and hosted a review visit in April-May 2006. The reviewers comprised an OECD Secretariat member, and academics and policy-makers from Australia, the United States, Finland, and the United Kingdom. The team is listed in Appendix 1.

1.2 The Participation of the Netherlands

The Netherlands' participation in the OECD Review was co-ordinated by Marlies Leegwater of the Netherlands Ministry of Education, Culture, and Science (OCW). Jos de Jonge and Jurriaan Berger of EIM prepared the Country Background Report (CBR) (OCW, 2006a) for the OECD Review (details are provided in Appendix 2).

---

[2]   The International Standard Classification of Education (ISCED) provides the foundation for internationally comparative education statistics and sets out the definitions and classifications that apply to educational programmes within it.

The review team is grateful to the authors of the CBR, and to all those who assisted them for providing an informative and policy-oriented document. The CBR covered themes such as the background and content of tertiary education reforms; the structure of the tertiary education system; the role of tertiary education in regional development, the research effort of the country; the shaping of labour markets; and the challenges faced in resourcing, governing, achieving equity in and assuring the quality of the tertiary education system.

The Netherlands CBR forms a valuable input to the overall OECD project and the review team found it to be very useful in relation to its work. The analysis and points raised in the CBR are cited frequently in this Country Note.[3] In this sense, the documents complement each other and, for a more comprehensive view of tertiary education policy in the Netherlands, are best read in conjunction.

The review visit took place from April 24-May 2 2006. An itinerary is provided in Appendix 3. The review team held discussions with educational authorities and relevant agencies and visited institutions of tertiary education in the country. Discussions were held with representatives of Ministries such as education and finance; tertiary education institutions; student organisations; representatives of academic staff; the business and industry community; and officials responsible for quality assurance. This allowed the team to obtain the views of key stakeholders in the system concerning the strengths, weaknesses, and policy priorities regarding tertiary education in the Netherlands.

This Country Note draws together the review team's observations and background materials. The present report on the Netherlands will be an input into the final OECD report on the overall project. The review team trusts that the Country Note will also contribute to discussions within the Netherlands, and inform the international education community about developments in the Netherlands that may hold lessons for their own systems.

The review team wishes to record its grateful appreciation to the many people who gave time from their busy schedules to assist in its work. The review team is grateful also for the informative and frank meetings that were held during the visit, and the helpful documentation provided by our hosts.

---

[3] Unless indicated otherwise, the data in this Country Note are taken from the Netherlands Country Background Report.

This Country Note is the responsibility of the review team. While the team benefited greatly from the Netherlands CBR and other documents, any errors or misinterpretations in this Country Note are its responsibility.

1.3 Structure of the Country Note

The remainder of the report is organised into ten chapters that focus on key issues within the scope of the review. Chapter Two provides a brief context and background of tertiary education in the Netherlands, Chapter Three reviews the governance of the tertiary system and its institutions. Chapters Four and Five examine the financing of the tertiary system and questions of equity, respectively. Chapter Six considers the linkages between tertiary education and labour markets in the Netherlands. Chapter Seven examines the role of tertiary education in research and innovation, while Chapter Eight examines policies and practices with respect to assuring and improving the quality of tertiary education. Issues of internationalisation of tertiary education are examined in Chapter Nine. Chapter Ten offers a brief conclusion. This is followed by a set of appendices.

2. *The Context and Background of Tertiary Education Policy in the Netherlands*

The Netherlands is a nation of 16.3 million people (2005). It has a small land area at 41 530 square kilometres, but has long been a major trading nation and is relatively wealthy: in 2005 per capita Gross National Income (GNI) was USD 32 480 in Purchasing Power Parity (PPP) terms, which was the tenth highest in the world when very small nations are excluded. In 2005 the GDP of the Netherlands was USD 537.7 billion in PPP terms, 22nd in the world and the sixth largest national product in Europe. In 2004 most of value added was in services (72.0% of GDP) followed by manufacturing at 25.6% and agriculture at just 2.4%. High technology exports constituted 29.1% of manufacturing exports (World Bank Data and Statistics, 2006).

The nation is strongly networked within the global communications system, providing global advantages for the nation in both business and higher education. In 2004 there were 524 Dutch Internet users per 1 000 population compared to an average of 480 in the World Bank's high-income group of countries. There were 190 broadband subscribers in the Netherlands compared to an average 126 in the high-income countries, and 992 mobile phone subscribers per 1000 people (World Bank, ICT data).

As is true elsewhere in Europe, the Netherlands has an ageing population, and the main source of demographic growth and the driver of future educational expansion is immigration. The number of inhabitants of 'non-Western' origin, principally from Northern Africa and the Middle East, is 10% overall but exceeds 30% in the four largest cities of Amsterdam, Rotterdam, The Hague and Utrecht. In these cities 51% of the population aged 0-14 are 'non-Western' (Background Report, p. 6). This group must figure largely in any policy consideration concerning tertiary education and poses issues in relation to social and cultural integration and the most effective use of human capital.

In 2004 the proportion of people aged 25-64 with tertiary qualifications was 29% compared to an OECD average of 25%. The level of qualifications in the Netherlands was below a number of high-income countries including Belgium, Scandinavia, the USA, Canada, Australia, Japan and Korea; but above the levels prevailing in Germany, France and the UK. The proportion of graduates in the 25-34 year old age group in the Netherlands (34%) is a little above the OECD average (31%). On this indicator the comparative position is stronger in the older age groups. In the 45-54 year old group the Netherlands proportion is 29% compared to an OECD average of 23%, a difference of six percentage points; in the 25-34 year old group the Netherlands proportion of 34% is only three percentage points above the OECD average of 31%. The fact that the participation gap between the Netherlands and the OECD average is moving towards closure in the younger age groups suggests that the bulk of OECD nations are improving participation more quickly than is the Netherlands. While the Netherlands continues to have a substantially larger share of young adults 25-34 with a long tertiary qualification than the OECD average (27% vs. 19%), it has only 2% of its 25-34 year old age cohort with a short tertiary qualification, as compared to 11 for the average OECD member country. The introduction of a two-year associate degree qualification is expected to narrow or eliminate this difference (OECD, 2006a, pp. 37-39).

Workforce participation by women is lower than in some other OECD nations, at 55% of those aged 15-64 years, and is concentrated in part-time work. Part-time work is increasing among men. However women continue to make advances in the professions and in 2002 held 25% of all positions in higher and scientific management compared to 14% in 1995 (Background Report, p. 7). The balance between women and men in higher education is roughly equal. As in most OECD nations the rate of entry of young women into first degrees considerably outstrips that of young men, while men constitute the larger group in doctoral programmes at a ratio of three to two.

In the Netherlands 86.1% of 15-19 year olds are enrolled in education, which is above the OECD average of 80.5% but on par with Western Europe. Participation of the 20-29 year age group in the Netherlands (25.5%) is just above the OECD average (24.7%). After 30 years age participation rates fall well below the OECD average, however. Just 2.9% of 30-39 year olds are enrolled in education as defined by OECD compared to 5.6% in the OECD as a whole, 15.6% in the UK and 13.5% in Sweden (OECD, 2006a, p. 266). This suggests that in the Netherlands there is a relatively weak commitment to lifelong learning and professional upgrading in the award programmes that have significant labour market cachet. This problem may be embedded in social culture, in that older people do not see award programmes in tertiary education as an option, but if so the incentive structure does not encourage a change of values. If they have not enrolled prior to 30 years of age higher education students lose their eligibility for student loans and some tuition charges rise steeply. More than in many other nations, in the Netherlands higher education is seen as the preserve of the young.

Higher education is based on a three-cycle degree system, consisting of Bachelor, Masters and PhD levels, in conformity with the Bologna model. The Netherlands has moved earlier and more comprehensively than most European nations in adopting this template though the transition is incomplete (Witte, 2006).

The two principal sectors of tertiary education are the research-intensive universities (the WOs) and the technical or 'professional' institutions, the *hogescholen* (the HBOs). There are 14 research-intensive universities including the Open University; eight academic medical centres and several publicly funded research institutes affiliated with the universities. There are 42 government funded HBOs. In recent years the HBO sector has become more concentrated via mergers and some of its institutions now enrol more than 30 000 students. The WOs and HBOs are separated on the basis of a division of labour (the 'binary system') in which the great majority of research functions and capacities are concentrated in the WOs. In contrast with academic staff at the research-intensive universities, few HBO staff hold doctoral degrees. On the whole HBO graduates are more specifically oriented to local and to occupationally tailored employment. There is a greater emphasis on generalist preparation in WOs. Organisationally, individual academic units within the WOs on the whole enjoy greater autonomy than their HBO counterparts. There are mergers and cooperation across the binary line but it is the subject of continuing policy tensions, particularly in relation to research and the funding of Masters programmes, as discussed in Chapter Three.

The total number of students in higher education in the Netherlands in 2005 was 546 400. Of these 199 300 students were enrolled in the research-intensive universities (the WOs) and 347, 100 in the HBOs (OCW, 2006b, pp. 81 and 97).

Beyond the binary system are designated (*aangewezen*) institutions. The operating costs of these institutions are not directly subsidised by the state; however, students eligible for publicly funded student grants and loans may use them to meet their study costs in accredited programmes at these institutions. There are nine institutes of this type at WO level and 62 at HBO level, typically quite small, enrolling a total of 60-70 000 students (Background Report, p. 13). Their share of total tertiary enrolments is just over 10%, and their role in the national system is modest.

There are an effective full-time 7 400 PhD students in Dutch universities and medical centres. In contrast with most other nations, being a doctoral student is a form of contract employment, normally for four years and including teaching duties. A small number of PhD students study on the basis of scholarships (Background Report, p. 16). Students graduate from advanced research programmes at an average age of 25 years, placing them as among the youngest in the OECD (OECD, 2005a, p. 422).

By international standards Dutch students are very well prepared for higher education. The nation is in the top group for mean levels of proficiency in the OECD PISA tests of mathematics and literacy among 15 year olds (*e.g.* for mathematics OECD, 2006a, p. 72). Overall performance is so high that even lower achieving school students in the Netherlands do quite well compared to students from other nations. Once Dutch students reach higher education they have a higher than OECD average completion rate, 76% compared to 71% (OECD, 2006a, pp. 99 and 59). This is a highly selected and culturally homogenous group by comparison with more open systems. Many potential degree students below the top group are weeded out at earlier stages.

Many secondary students are not destined for higher education. During secondary school, beginning at 12 years, students are streamed into three hierarchically ordered groups on the basis of academic potential: the VWO, the stream constituting the pathway to research intensive universities (the WOs), though some go the HBOs; the HAVO which provides students for the HBOs or MBO vocational training at tertiary stage; and the VMBO which prepares students solely for MBO tertiary training. In total about 60% of students enrolled in upper secondary education are in vocational programmes; and at the level of higher education about two thirds of all students are enrolled in the HBOs rather than the research-intensive universities. Both the proportion of secondary students in vocational programmes, and the proportion of tertiary students in non-doctoral 'professional universities' (HBOs) rather than the research intensive academic universities which enjoy the highest per capita funding and social status, are much higher than the OECD averages. This includes other nations such as Finland and Germany with binary systems (for more discussion see Chapters Five-Six).

Students selected for the VWO stream tend to have very favourable outcomes. All who qualify for entrance to the research-intensive universities are accepted; most are able to enter into their first choice programme. When applications exceed the planned number of places the universities have the choice of either expanding the enrolment beyond the planned level, or conducting a process of selection. In some faculties (*i.e.* medicine) selection is highly determined by ballot. During year 1 all students are advised on their subsequent studies. At this stage some will be excluded from further progression in their chosen programme. Thus the end of the first year is often the decisive moment when the future pathway is determined.

Nevertheless, once designated for the academic stream in secondary school, nearly all those so selected remain in it; and in that stream they are relatively well supported. The Netherlands spends a relatively high USD 70 932 per average student enrolled in the OECD category of tertiary type A and advanced research programmes, over the duration of the course of study. Thus the Netherlands combines a middling level of overall spending and participation with the concentration of tertiary enrolments at degree programme level and relatively generous support for the top group of students in the research intensive universities who are better resourced than in most other countries (OECD, 2006a). The student loans system is also relatively generous to those eligible for it. However the situation is different for those streamed below VWO level while at secondary school, whether in the VMBO or HAVO streams. Arguably, the three-track structure of secondary schooling inhibits the capacity of the Netherlands to lift total participation in the research-intensive universities and HBOs, especially participation and subsequent completion among the immigrant communities whose school students are disproportionately streamed into the VMBO group. This became a primary concern of the team during the review (see Chapter Five).

With the exception of the top echelon of academic research, higher education institutions are not exposed to a high level of open competition; and if they were it is unclear how they would respond. The HBO focus on the local employment destinations of graduates raises questions about the national and international mobility of those graduates. HBO instructors are less academically trained than are those in the higher professional education sectors in Germany and Finland.

The Ministry of OCW (Education, Culture and Science) administers most government higher education programmes. Other departments also play a role, particularly in relation to research and innovation, including the Ministry of Economic Affairs. There are on-going issues of coordination and cooperation within and between the ministries involved. In 2003 the Netherlands spent just 5.0% of GDP on education compared to the OECD country average of 5.9%. Both public funding of education in the Netherlands (4.6% compared to the OECD average of 5.2%) and private funding (0.4% compared to 0.7%) fell below the OECD mean. At tertiary level the comparative picture is somewhat stronger. Total financing of tertiary education at 1.3% of GDP was only just below the OECD average of 1.4%. Public funding was at the OECD average level of 1.1% while private funding (0.3%) was a little below the OECD indicator (0.4%). A worrying sign is that between 1995 and 2003 total Dutch spending on tertiary education from public and private sources increased by just 12% compared to the OECD average of 46% and an EU-19 average of 47% (OECD, 2006a, pp. 191, 205, 208-209).

The Netherlands is a modest national investor in R&D given its total level of economic resources. The nation spent 1.80% of GDP on R&D in 2002, compared to an OECD average of 2.26%. Investment in R&D in the research intensive universities is stronger in comparative terms than is business R&D. Company expenditure on R&D of 0.90% of GDP in 2002 was well below the OECD average of 1.40%, while Dutch public spending on R&D of 0.67% in 2002 was on par with the OECD average of 0.68%. Correspondingly the Netherlands is stronger in basic research indicators than in innovation indicators. Dutch scientific publications constituted a high 2.45% of the world total in 2001 (data supplied by NWO and the Ministry of Education, Culture and Science). As noted the research intensive universities are strong in international terms, but despite rather than because of the system of incentives operating at the national level (see Chapter Three).

The 2006 OECD *Economic Survey* of the Netherlands noted that the nation 'has an excellent record in knowledge creation but a mediocre record in innovation activity, which is defined as the successful development and application of knowledge in new products and/or processes'. The rate of scientific publications per capita is the sixth highest in the OECD and these publications have an excellent citation impact. But the nation ranks only 12th on the 2004 EIS Summary Innovation Index, well below the leaders (pp. 104-106). In policy circles in the Netherlands this is dubbed the 'Dutch paradox'; though the problem is also more general to Western Europe and is also known as the 'European paradox'. The 'paradox' in the Netherlands in part derives from the industry structure: the Netherlands is primarily a service economy and there is a limited number of large scale firms requiring R&D. The 'paradox' has stimulated a broad range of policy schemes, instruments and funding incentives that are designed to stimulate innovation and sustain industry-university and public-private partnerships. These are discussed in Chapter Seven.

The Country Background Report for this review concluded that the Netherlands secures a good quality and quantity of 'outputs' for a relatively modest national funding outlay, though the proportion of students who graduate, and the speed of their graduation, could be better. 'Good value for money is one of the main characteristics of the entire system' (p. 93). Good value for money is a commendable quality, and it has deep roots in the Dutch culture. However, good value for money can be had at any level of performance, and it is a criterion that carries with it the risk of inducing national complacency.

We propose a different measure of achievement, in which the public and political leaders ask "is our tertiary system sufficient to meet the demands of a more European and global future, in which we must become a leading knowledge economy – and at the same time able to assist in the integration of first and second generation immigrant populations into the human capital and culture of the nation?"

3. System and Institutional Governance

3.1 Background

The Netherlands aspires to use its tertiary education resources to help it move into a European leadership position among knowledge-based economies by 2010. The government has strategies to achieve this goal, set out in policy documents such as the *Hoger Onderwijs en Onderzoek Plan* (HOOP) 2004. Four ministries – Finance, Economic Affairs, Education, Culture, and Science and Agriculture, Nature and Food Quality – are involved in formulating and executing tertiary education policy and resourcing toward this end.

The primary responsibility for national funding, programmes and policy advice in higher education is assumed by the Ministry of OCW (Education, Culture and Science). The Ministry was recently reorganised to combine the units responsible for research-intensive universities and HBOs. In the process the number of OCW tertiary education staff was reduced from 140 to 70 (Interview with Erik Martijnse, CHEPS, 2006, p. 4). This reorganisation may have affected programme capacity in specific areas during the period of the visit by the review team. The ministry of Agriculture, Nature and Food Quality is responsible for the institutions within the domain of agriculture and natural environment.

In 2003 the felt need to accelerate innovation processes in the Netherlands, the 'silo' character of programme administration and the need for closer coordination of education, research and industry policy in key areas prompted the initiation of the Innovation Platform by the Prime Minister. This is a cross-portfolio task force with membership from the Ministries of Economic Affairs and Education, Culture and Science, leading companies such as Philips and Shell, and personnel from the research sector (see also Chapter Seven).

The research-intensive universities (WOs) are specifically funded for research both through their general government grant and again through competitive programmes. This ensures that their unit resource position is stronger than that of the *hogescholen* (HBOs), which educate the majority of students. The HBOs have a restricted power to award degrees and are not fully funded by government for programmes at Masters level, though they offer some professional and research Masters programmes and would like to expand these activities.

In national binary systems tradition and reality do not always coincide. The traditional wisdom is that the HBOs are associated with the preparation of students for work in smaller and localised enterprises, and also for professions (Background Report, p. 76), suggesting that graduates are heading for locally rooted professions; while by implication research intensive university graduates are more broadly prepared. In practice this does not effectively distinguish the HBOs from the research-intensive universities. Labour markets are increasingly mobile and career changes during a working lifetime increasingly frequent. Graduates from either sector can work in enterprises of varying size and varying degrees of local orientation. Dutch graduates from either sector are now more likely than before to work across the Netherlands, across Europe and elsewhere in the world. Research-intensive universities prepare professionals in some fields and, like HBOs, could expand their role in shorter programmes and continuing education. Like research-intensive universities although less so, HBOs offer some programmes with a generic content. There is overlap in business, law and communications. Some HBOs would like to expand their role in Arts/Science degrees.

It might be possible to distinguish the sectors more precisely on the basis of the occupations and industries they respectively prepare, but such a distinction would blur in places and would be more arbitrary than foundational. Rather, it is research that provides a clear-cut distinction. Only the WOs have a significant involvement in internationally competitive basic research and doctoral programmes, and have a high proportion of research-qualified staff. The HBOs have some involvement in research processes: they have access to R&D support through the *lectoren* programme (see Chapter Seven) and would like to extend their research activities but they do not maintain a significant basic research capacity. Currently only 5% of HBO staff hold doctoral qualifications and few HBO staff currently publish in internationally recognised research journals at scale. Because many HBO faculty members prefer to write in Dutch rather than the English used in international journals, the HBOs are considering a reward system encompassing HBO-based definitions of publication and research impact.

However it is defined, the present binary line is not fully stable. The HBO-Raad advocates the expansion of funded Masters by research and Arts/Science degrees in the HBOs; and individual HBOs want more funding for research activities. Although it was never put to the review team in quite those terms, these proposals appeared designed to secure closer parity with the research-intensive universities, in terms of status and resources. Perhaps research funding is seen as key to closing the resources gap between the sectors. Likewise some in the HBOs see the *lectoren* programme not so much as a means of developing teaching-driven research and consultancy functions in the SMEs, so much as the beach-head for a research role paralleling that of the WOs. The research-intensive universities are concerned that the binary system may break down if such changes go ahead. At the same time their own forays into professional and occupationally targeted programmes, to secure the funding generated by student numbers, might be converging with the role of the HBOs as popularly understood. These are all signs of impending academic 'drift' that, if unchecked, could undermine the rationale for and the structural supports of the binary distinction. If policy makers remained committed to the binary line they need to reconsider the several and mutual operations of the two sectors and to monitor the binary line on an ongoing basis.

Binary systems based on a limited and fixed diversification can work only if institutions are not permitted to change mission/profile outside the basic parameters of their mutually exclusive roles. Such systems require constant policing. The alternative is to move towards a more flexible single system permitting substantial variations in mission/profile. After the UK and Australia abolished their binary systems there was a tendency to convergence around the single template of research university comprehensive across the fields of study. Arguably this foreshadowed a larger number of research intensive universities than either nation needed; and in fact both national systems contain a substantial number of universities in which doctoral training and basic research are not fully established in all fields. The British Research Assessment Exercise and the current Australian policy of fostering greater diversity through university-driven missions now point towards a pattern of more complex and diverse specialisations within the national system. In both nations several types of institution have emerged on an informal basis with self-managed groupings.

Though binary systems have been abolished in some nations they remain successful in others. The German *Fachhochschulen* have secured an international standing in excess of that of the Dutch HBOs. Doctoral qualifications are normal among faculty in the *Fachhochschulen* though the institutions are not funded for research on the scale of the academic universities. The German vocational model, including the mechanisms used to involve industry, cannot be replicated in the Netherlands as Germany has a more manufacturing–based economy. However the principles of near-parity of esteem and parity of academic qualifications might be worth imitating. Finland has also established a strong polytechnic sector that enabled the doubling of higher education enrolments between 1990 and 2000. The polytechnics are distinguished on the basis of shorter study programmes, a more technically oriented and applied approach, more input into governance from employers and local and regional authorities, and a greater element of localised financing (OECD, 2006b, pp. 121-122). Finland now appears to be moving towards a more flexible binary system in which the degree and type of diversification is managed according to judgments about national and regional needs. A feature of the Finnish system is the encouragement given to shared facilities, programmes and marketing across the binary divide. Some proposals for limited mergers are also under consideration. In the Netherlands WO/HBO mergers have become a chief mechanism for creating flexibility and sustaining growth. However, in the context of a tightly defined binary divide, without the formal mandating of flexibility and variety within and across the sectors, such cross-binary activity can compound the confusion of roles and expectations.

In the top echelon of academic research the best Dutch researchers and scholars compete directly with the rest of the world in what has become a global knowledge system. The quality and quantity of research in the research intensive universities is testified by international comparisons of publication and citations across all broad discipline groups, with Dutch research in Medicine a standout area; and though there is continuing scope for improvement, the nation can be proud of its achievements in this regard, which provide a solid floor for the national innovation system. Nevertheless there are some indications that Netherlands research is less than fully competitive as a national system *qua* system. The spirit of excellence tends to be concentrated at the top of the academic profession, the part directly involved in international research at the highest level, rather than permeating the whole of localised research and scholarly activity. Voluntary cultures of academic excellence are better at driving high performance among the best researchers than in the whole of a knowledge system. Given the present incentive structure it is doubtful that the Netherlands can attract enough strong foreign researchers to compensate for the front rank Dutch researchers who leave the country. Further, though NWO funding is allocated on the basis of merit, competitive pressures in the research funding component of the basic grant are muted. That part of basic research funding that is performance-related is provided in the form of lump sums to the universities so that there is no guarantee that it will be internally allocated to the reinforcement of research capacity rather than, say, plugging holes in resources for teaching, administration or other facilities. Thus the linkage between research performance and research funding is not guaranteed. This undermines the capacity of the performance-related funding to drive performance. Only with a minority of research funding, that allocated on a programme and project basis by NWO, is the full force of national competition brought to bear on research funding and a clear-cut linkage created between research merit and resource support.

In the student markets, where there is no equivalent of the drive for top-level research excellence, competitive pressures are weaker than in research. The HBOs have no obvious international competitor for their student market. The research-intensive universities have a guaranteed student 'market' as well. There is no systematic evidence on the quality of teaching in either sector: no one knows if this is improving or declining. In response to its concerns on the point of teaching quality, the review team was provided with data on employment rates of graduates, and on the accreditation process. While graduate employability is in itself a relevant indicator, especially from the point of view of graduates themselves, it cannot answer the need for data on teaching quality. Employment rates do not distinguish between educational effects and labour market effects.

It is a truth universally acknowledged in the research-intensive universities, one also emphasised to the review team by VNO-NCW, that Dutch universities must position themselves in the international context. The culture of internationally competitive research excellence is formally grounded in the Netherlands through the process of accreditation of 'excellent' research schools and the involvement of foreign peers in the regular quality assurance of research schools (Background Report, p. 77; see Chapter Seven). Some national research schemes turn on competition between bids for support of projects and individuals, though the majority of performance based funding continues to be allocated within the block grant, which retards direct competition on the basis of excellence. In general direct competitive pressures and allocations are shaped more on a disciplinary basis than an institutional basis. The new question at issue is the potential of material resource concentrations on an institution-wide basis, interacting with the status driver typical of elite research universities, to strengthen the world competitive position of research in the Netherlands.

For better or worse the present global standing of Dutch universities is reflected in, and to a degree formed by, their position in the two sets of world university rankings issued annually by Shanghai Jiao Tong University (commenced in 2003) and the *Times Higher Education Supplement* (commenced in 2004).[4] Dutch universities do fairly well under both

---

[4] The global university rankings issued by *Newsweek* are not separate rankings in their own right, they are a scissors and tape combination of part of the Shanghai Jiao Tong rankings, part of the *Times* ranking, with the addition of data on library holdings. In content that are closer to the Jiao Tong data in that they are largely grounded in research and publication (*Newsweek,* 'The world's most global universities', 21-28 August, 2006, pp. 36-66).

measures. Of the two the more significant data are the Shanghai Jiao Tong rankings that are transparent, based on credible metrics and focused on research, the main signifier of the standing of university activities worldwide. The bulk of the Shanghai Jiao Tong index is determined by publication and citation, principally in the science-based disciplines with some attention to social sciences and humanities: 20% citation in leading journals; 20% articles in *Science* and *Nature*; and 20% the number of Thomson/ISI 'HiCi' researchers on the basis of citation (Institute for Scientific Information, 2006). Another 30% is determined by the winners of Nobel Prizes in the sciences and economics and Fields Medals in mathematics, based on the location of training (10%) and current employment (20%). The remaining 10% is determined by dividing the total derived from the above data by the number of faculty.

Jiao Tong research performance is dominated by the English speaking nations, which have 71% of the world's top 100 research universities, and particularly by the United States which has 17 of the top 20 and 54 of the top 100 in 2006. The Netherlands has two universities in the Shanghai Jiao Tong world's top 100 - the University of Utrecht at number 40 and the University of Leiden at 72 - and seven universities in the top 200, which includes Amsterdam, Groningen, Delft, the Free University Amsterdam and Wageningen. On this measure the Netherlands is sixth nation in the world after the USA (87 universities in the top 200), the UK (22), Germany (15), Japan (9) and Canada (8) and just ahead of France, Switzerland, Australia and Italy with six universities each; although France, Switzerland and Sweden all have more universities than does the Netherlands in the Jiao Tiong top 100. In total the Netherlands has 12 universities in the full Jiao Tong top 500: the remaining five are Erasmus University in Rotterdam, Nijmegen, TU Eindhoven, Maastricht and TU Twente (Shanghai Jiao Tong University Institute of Higher Education, 2006).

An institution and nation's performance in the Jiao Tong ranking is affected by the presence of 'HiCi' researchers classified by Thomson/ISI as among the top 250-300 in their field worldwide. 3 614 of the Thomson/ISI 'HighCi' researchers are in the USA, compared to 224 in Germany, 138 in France, 94 in Switzerland and 55 in Sweden. There are 90 in the Netherlands. In comparison Harvard and its affiliated institutes have 168 HiCi researchers, Stanford has 132, and the University of Cambridge in the UK has 42. In the Netherlands Leiden has 15 HiCi researchers, Utrecht 14, Wageningen 13 and the Free University 10 (Institute for Scientific Information, 2006). Table 3.1 provides details:

Table 3.1: Dutch Universities in The Shanghai Jiao Tong University Ranking of The World's Top 500 Research Universities, 2006

	Position in Jiao Tong University rankings	Number of Thomson/ISI 'HiCi' researchers
Utrecht	40	14
Leiden	72	15
Amsterdam	102-150	6
Groningen	102-150	4
TU Delft	151-200	1
Free University Amsterdam	151-200	10
Wageningen	151-200	13
Erasmus, Rotterdam	201-300	5
Nijmegen	201-300	1
TU Eindhoven	301-400	0
Maastricht	301-400	1
TU Twente	301-400	2
Other researcher locations	n.a.	18

n.a. = not applicable

From the point of view of system organisation, the question now posed by world rankings is whether, and if so to what extent, government should pursue a deliberate policy of concentration of resources and activities, particularly in research, so as to enable the top research universities to compete on more equal terms with the English-speaking nations. Front rank universities are strong global magnets for high calibre researchers, doctoral students, public research funding from different nations, and corporate investors in university research located anywhere in the world. All else being equal, the location in the Netherlands of several universities with the research and status firepower of Oxford or Yale would significantly increase national capacity within the global knowledge economy; although in itself it would not guarantee that this enhanced capacity would necessarily be directed to national economic objectives. A number of national governments are currently considering the potential offered by policies of concentration on an institutional basis, notably Germany, Japan, and China. This is distinct from policies that seek to achieve a national division of labour by distributing high-level research specialisations between different universities by field. By concentrating across-the-board strength in a small number of universities the potential inter-disciplinary synergies are maximised, the climate of excellence is enhanced with positive effects everywhere, and the factor of institutional status (the 'brand') is deployed to maximum national and global advantage.

On the other hand, those national governments that go down this road will want to avoid weakening existing research capacity and morale in institutions not chosen for front rank status. A broad-based national research capacity is also an advantage in the global context. It would be better to proceed by adding new resources to the designated institutions, rather than a zero-sum distribution which may leave the national system no better off overall.

In some respects the structure of institution-government relations in the Netherlands is closer to that of the UK than the public service administrations of much of Europe. The model has been described as 'state supervision' rather than 'state control' (Background Report, p. 72). Since the WHW Law on higher education first issued in 1992 institutions have enjoyed a relatively high level of autonomy. They receive a block grant from government based on a transparent formula, own their buildings and appoint professors; though Ministerial permission is required to move into a new location or offer a programme that may be duplicated elsewhere. Institutional control over student numbers is limited by the fact that they must admit all students with the required secondary school certificate, though limits can be set in particular subjects (Background Report, pp. 71-72). In the research intensive universities there is external accreditation rather than self-accreditation. As in many other national systems, in recent years central government has exerted a greater authority via accountability requirements. It seems this is driven more by avoidance of risk than by desire to closely shape the product of higher education.

Recent experiments in institution-government relations tend towards a more market-like system, for example through tuition price variation. There is merit in measures that open up a more diverse range of provision and of approaches to existing provision, provided that the incentives point providers, consumers and community and industry users of higher education towards excellence and innovation, *e.g.* rather than institutions competing on the basis of price cutting in standardised programmes. Measures opening up a more active role for student decision-making; and/or encourage higher levels of student achievement are especially welcome. At this stage these policy experiments have had minor effects in the system as a whole. (More is said about this area below and Chapter Four).

In the research-intensive universities funding for research is provided via three mechanisms or 'streams'. Stream 1, constituting approximately 60% of all support for research, is intended to provide for basic research infrastructure including personnel costs. Stream 1 is comprised by both a performance-related component and another component known as the Strategic Considerations Component. It is provided on the basis of block funding. Stream 2, approximately 10% of research funding in total, consists of funding allocated on academic grounds by the principal research funding agency, based on evaluation of research excellence and competitive funding for projects and programmes. The remaining 30% of research funding in Stream 3 is monies for research conducted for government departments, consultancy income, philanthropic foundations, European sources, etc. (OCW, 2004a, p. 19). Institutions are required to support Stream 2 and 3 allocations with a portion of their Stream 1 monies. One problem that has arisen is that under this formula certain institutions whose incomes under Streams 2 and 3 exceed income under Stream 1 have a disincentive to seek further Stream 2 funding (see Chapter Seven).

Currently almost 60% of total university funding is performance-based and this will rise to about two thirds when the Smart-Mix component is added (see Chapter Seven). About half of all university researchers are now paid from Streams 2 and 3 (AWT, 2005, p. 3). The three-tier structure allows government and national research agencies to influence the flow of activities by varying the performance-related components, and varying the rules governing the relationship between Stream 1 and the other Streams. 'There are already a lot of incentives in university research... the (university) research sector is one of the most competitive sectors of Dutch society' (p. 10). On the other hand, as noted the proportion of research funding that is allocated by direct competition for specific support on grounds of excellence – the 10% in Stream 2 - is relatively low.

The institutional governance of the WOs and HBOs is distinctive to the Netherlands and might constitute a useful option for other nations to consider. The Executive Board structure based on three key executive personnel (typically designated as Rector; President; and Vice-President, Vice-Rector or simply as third member of the Executive Board) constitutes a structure of distributed leadership with less dependence on and pressure on a single pivotal authority. The Executive Board structure allows part of the institutional executive to be appointed from outside the university while balancing this with leaders drawn from faculty ranks; and is capable of a broad range of variations in the division of portfolios, and the internal/external balance of responsibilities. It can be shaped around the particular strengths of the individuals concerned and/or the strategic needs of the institution at a particular time. It is possible for the authority of two positions to be combined in one individual, thereby approximating the CEO role without installing such a function on a permanent basis.

The Supervisory Board consists of a range of personnel with professional, industry, governmental and academic expertise. This structure allows the institution to mobilise a range of constituencies as constructive contributors to governance, while anchoring the institution more firmly. This has an often and particularly local utility in the HBOs but is at least as equally important in the research universities in providing lines of accountability to industry and community. On the evidence available to the Review team, both the structure and culture of Supervisory Boards is effective. In the institutions visited, it was reported that the Boards become usefully involved in the institution while respecting academic freedoms and executive prerogatives. The Supervisory Boards may also serve as a training ground for some outside personnel who are subsequently appointed to Executive Board positions.

Both types of institutions provide employees and students with an advisory voice in governance and management and at field of study level. Student involvement in decision-making has been framed at a more advanced level compared to most other higher education systems. One problem is that it can be difficult to secure the participation of sufficient numbers of personnel and students in active roles within the structures (Background Report, p. 75).

At the level of fields of study, in the research universities the Faculty Deanship operates in a manner more similar to academic bodies in other nations, while the HBO director functions more like a manager in a traditionally managerial organization. The Deanship varies in term of office and, method of appointment, the extent to which the dean is full-time, and the extent to which he/she is drawn into central institutional governance. Institutions also vary in the extent to which internal allocations are performance-related, central authorities can generate initiatives and/or retire fields at faculty level, and non-faculty staff are administered at central or faculty levels.

3.2 Strengths

Higher education in the Netherlands is stable, well rooted in the history and culture of the nation. Governance, regulation and management being partly formal and partly customary, are well understood by practitioners at all levels. Arguably the primary strengths of higher education in the Netherlands lie in its functioning at institutional level, especially but not only in the stronger research universities; and these institutional virtues are sustained by what is on the whole a successful day-to-day relationship between government and institutions based on a relatively low level of interference. At both national and institutional levels, the weight of the system on its component parts is less heavy and arbitrary than in many other countries. These are favourable conditions for the core businesses of teaching and occupational preparation, research and consultancy, and community services.

Although governance is not always transparent, geographical proximity helps ensure that all parts of the system are aware of and accessible to each other, and are known to and know of national government. These virtues are particularly manifest in the systems of research support. The set of schemes for fostering university-industry cooperation is perhaps unduly complex (see Chapter Seven) but sustains an intensive level of networking and mutual understanding that helps to drive high basic research performance.

There are established traditions of institutional autonomy, sub-institutional autonomy and academic freedom, more so in the research universities than in the HBOs. Perhaps the governance model works a little better in the research intensive universities for this reason, given the decentralised character of faculty cultures, and authority that is often scholarly rather than bureaucratic, providing that formal and informal performance drivers establish an adequate framework of incentives. The governance model is optimised in institutions where decentralised academic agency operates in tandem with central executive systems for steering priorities and monitoring performance that are tailored so as to fit each field of activity.

At the institutional level the temper of governance on the whole is modest, consultative and democratic. Little energy is wasted in symbolic posturing and conflict. People get on with the job.

There are also well established habits of cooperation throughout higher education, as evidenced for example in the collaboration between the technical universities, the merger negotiations between research universities and HBOs, and the operations of agencies such as TNO that work across sector boundaries. Another example is the cooperation between the Wageningen University, the agricultural HBOs and Agricultural Education Centers (offering vocational and pre-vocational education) within the domain of agriculture and natural environment. These institutions together form the "Groene kenniscoöperatie". Though there are tensions in the binary line, some tensions are inevitable in any binary system.

Another strength is that at times the national authorities make effective use of disinterested expertise in policy making. One example is the Advisory Council for Science and Technology Policy, which has a mandate to provide government and parliament with long-term strategic advice, and is independent of both government and the higher education institutions. Another is the Committee on the dynamics of university research, the Chang committee (see Ministry of Economic Affairs, 2006, p. 28) which looked critically at components of the innovation system. Not all national governments are willing to use experts creatively in this way. At times the government also makes effective use of foreign expertise, for example in the evaluation of policy tools and programmes; as indeed the government welcomed this thematic OECD review by an external team.

The distinctive structure of governance at institutional level, with Executive Boards and Supervisory Boards, has significant strengths and as noted it is one that other nations might consider.

3.3 Weaknesses

Based on the evidence of the interviews and consultations during the review visit, the review team concludes that although they are said to be important national goals, the Lisbon targets appear to be given 'lip-service' more than effective and practical commitment. We suspect that this is an example of a more general problem. It seems that the practical implications of national goals in tertiary education, in the areas of priorities, resources and the transformation of practices and cultures, are rarely analysed or acknowledged. In other words, such goals appear to operate largely at the rhetorical level and as part of the 'noise' of electoral politics, with not much urgency about implementation. If this is so, it is a key weakness in the capacity of the higher education system *qua* system.

While the work of tertiary institutions is often good, this happens despite rather than because of the national policy framework and incentives. The primary weaknesses in governance and management are found at the national level, in system policy and steering. The review team became especially concerned about the handling of strategic direction and new policy initiatives at OCW (with the partial exception of the policy field of research and innovation, much of which lies outside OCW). In many respects Dutch higher education system appears to be on 'auto-pilot'. The capacity (and perhaps willingness) of government to provide executive leadership so as to shape the system in the national interest, including global competitiveness and trajectory, appears under-developed. Some initiatives that *are* taken appear to be a case of being seen to do something, rather than addressing real problems with real solutions. These weaknesses, some of which may have their roots in the larger policy/political culture of which OCW is only one part, retard the capacities of nation and institutions to respond to contemporary challenges. One example is the OCW-generated bill on higher education that was under discussion at the time of the review team's visit. This had been canvassed in the normal manner with stakeholders, reflected discussions between different ministries with an interest in higher education, and contained new initiatives. However, arguably, it did not reflect a process of consultation that was sustained or deep, nor did it go to the root of the problems of Dutch tertiary education, nor did it contribute to the building of a policy consensus for new solutions that would be effective and lasting rather than tentative and symbolic. Here we are not making an argument for more centralised and still less for more bureaucratic approaches to government, which would retard rather than enhance global competence. Rather, the need is for a *strategically effective devolution*: for a more functional, goal driven relationship between responsive local institutional autonomy, system culture and national executive strategy. This is likely to mean more local autonomy not less, and less central bureaucracy not more - but also greater transparency at all levels, and a more strategic approach to policy. And it should also add up to improved system and institutional performance in the relation to the big national performance goals such has the Lisbon targets, global competitiveness, and the inclusion of immigration-based communities. It is the long-term outcomes that matter. Here we would contrast the more reactive approach taken by OCW to the strategic and long-term thinking exhibited by policy makers in rising Asian science powers such as Singapore, Korea and China.

Inter-departmental and intra-departmental coherence also could be improved. For example, the Economic Departments of government have important policy ideas in relation to higher education, and the capacity to work across different portfolio areas so as to integrate Education more effectively into national priorities. The OCW has the main executive responsibility in relation to education programmes but does not command the policy power of the economic ministries and perhaps this overall division of labour contributes to the limitations of governmental leadership in tertiary education. Based upon conversations with civil servants and higher education institutions, the review team developed the impression that Ministry of Education officials sometimes viewed the interventions of other Ministries, such as the Ministry of Economic Affairs, as a threat to its role in directing higher education policy. Rather than departments responding defensively (or aggressively) it would be better to coordinate more effectively. There also appears to be room for improved coordination between on one hand the arms of government responsible for education, and on the other hand the arms of government responsible for immigration and services for immigrant populations.

An attitude change is needed but equally important are formal mechanisms for coordination. Forms of cross-departmental organization and cooperation, such as the Innovation Platform - which was created as a combined initiative of OCW and Economic Affairs led by the Prime Minister - can play a significant role. In the case of the Innovation Platform, its impact is limited by its temporary nature, and its partial composition on the basis of interests, and the distance between it and programme implementation.

Inside the OCW the division of labour is not always stable, integrating mechanisms across bureaux or work units appear to be insufficient, and the level of experience in key eras can be highly uneven. The OCW appears to lack sufficient personnel with a close knowledge of the inside workings of tertiary institutions, for example those who have worked as faculty or in university administration. The Inspectorate does not seem well integrated with other operations.

It seems that decisions are often 'guided' by short-term factors, and not robust and transparent long-term planning agendas. Perhaps OCW lacks the capacity to establish genuine operational priorities and focus, and to push for greater excellence in a determined way in defined areas so as to achieve clearly identified outcomes. Our judgement here is that the OCW tends to reflect the ebb and flow of currents and tensions in the sector, and in the larger policy/political environment, rather than being a point where these currents and tensions are resolved. While an element of short-term responsiveness is an inevitable and desirable part of democratic government, the key issue is how short-term and long-term agendas are managed in relation to each other, so as to keep the longer-term policy objectives in sight. We would expect that a department of government - as distinct from the office of the Minister - should be a voice for policy rather than politics, and should carry a brief not for the quick fix but for the long term health and effectiveness of the system for which it is responsible. The result of being more responsive than responsible is that the policy position of the Ministry is not always transparent, and in some cases there is no policy. This has created uncertainty in higher education institutions and their representative organizations about 'what the government thinks'. We emphasise that we are not imagining or intuiting this problem. The point about 'what the government thinks' was made frequently to the review team during the review visits, and was heard in government agencies as well as in discussions with the institutions and the stakeholder organisations.

More attention needs to be given to the development of best practice instruments competent to formulate, initiate, steer, monitor and evaluate in the national interest. Correspondingly, data collections are not fully transparent, and data capacity in certain key areas is poor, for example cross-border faculty movement; cross-border movements of doctoral students and postdoctoral scholar-researchers; research and consultancy activities in the third stream of research funding; the distribution of first stream research funding within institutional budgets; and the long-term career trajectories of those who graduate from WO and HBO institutions. The more decentralised English-speaking systems have created high quality comprehensive data collections, often via accountability requirements. These data collections are essential to steering instruments that are consistent with self-management and operate at a distance.

Likewise, the Netherlands would benefit from a stronger practice of policy experimentation, for example in the use of pilot schemes, and bid-based opportunities to create new initiatives from below.

Within a binary system that is marked by a high degree of uniformity within each segment, formula-based resource allocation to and within institutions, and a student market with little dynamism, higher education practices are perhaps too uniform and predictable. This is the downside of the benefits of stability. There is an under-developed capacity to steer, reorient and reinvent practice in response to changing needs, for example the emerging requirements created by global competition and European labour mobility. Executive steering at one level cannot always compensate for deficiencies in the other. Many other higher education systems have a stronger steering capacity at government level, institutional level, or both.

The requirement that the Ministry sign off on new programmes seems inconsistent with the broader pattern of university autonomy and tends to inhibit innovation. While the intention is to avoid duplication, monopolistic specialisation does not always produce optimum results. Even in similar programmes competitive pressures and the aggregation of best practice experience can be productive, especially where diverse approaches are generated. Rather than attempting to sort these possibilities from the ministerial office it would seem better to allow evolution to take its course, with the exception of specific areas such as Dentistry and Medicine where the rationing of provision and centrally determined specialisation are necessary for both economic and professional reasons. This issue is further addressed in Chapter Eight.

The binary line provides for two sectors with distinct roles but neither is functioning at optimum level; nor does the fairly inflexible binary structure enable the fullest range of national needs to be met. The research intensive universities are relatively strong in basic research and find it relatively easy to educate their relatively homogenous clientele, but their relationship with students is provider-pastoral rather than student-driven and given the mechanisms of funding and enrolment the adequacy of teaching and support services is untested through the rigours of competition. The HBO system, though now mature, is not perceived internationally as a benchmark or model of higher professional education. This seems to be the result, in part, of the low intensity of doctoral training among its staff, and an orientation that is often exclusively local – rather than focused on a vista that is global, national *and* local. The HBO public mission as small employer and teaching-oriented institutions - and the structure of the educational marketplace in the Netherlands - protects them from systematic scrutiny and competition on these national and international dimensions. Given these policy frameworks neither sector is guaranteed to be competitive in the recruitment of foreign students or to respond to the substantial challenges of modernisation, global competition and immigrant populations. In addition to the two principal sectors there is a small number of *aangewezen instellingen*, private institutions with the authority to award degrees. These have a very small enrolment share and do not constitute substantial system diversity or provide meaningful competitive pressure for the WOs and HBOs.

There is insufficient scope across the system for diversification and specialisation. Differences in mission and *modus operandi* are restricted to those flowing from the binary line and this is relatively inflexible. Without more diversity within each segment, a renovation of the HBOs to reflect a more modernised and global service economy, and more active relationships between institutions and their student and employer markets, the binary system constitutes a limited, inflexible division of labour.

Just as the weakness of direct competition for research programme and project funding diminishes the potential for excellence in the research system, so the absence of a genuine market in teaching inhibits both excellence and client-oriented diversity in that sphere. The funding and enrolment system creates certain perverse incentives that work against both excellence and diversity of programme and mission, such as the combination of guaranteed local entry to specified 'seats' and the boosting of student numbers beyond capacity to augment income. The absence of tuition price variation in most programmes means that it is difficult for institutions to create 'lighthouse' programmes with high quality or distinctive new mission.

The outcome is that while institutions enjoy an appropriate level of operational autonomy, public authorities have failed to create a policy framework in which tertiary education institutions can fully exploit that autonomy through innovation and client-oriented specialisation, and external drivers can be brought to bear on the institutions so as to entrench them in national priorities and local needs.

In addition the system is largely closed to foreign institutions, despite the facts that they might offer valid educational opportunities for Dutch citizen students, and some Dutch citizens already go abroad for higher education or access foreign study via the Internet. Webster University in Leiden and the University of Phoenix in Rotterdam are not included within the national regulatory framework, including the requirements for accreditation and quality assurance, although they recruit Dutch students.

Another sub-set of the segmentation and diversity issue is the question of possible 'super-league' institutions. Although the quality of basic research in Dutch universities is very good overall, and all research universities contribute to this, at this stage the nation has not developed outstanding individual research universities that are comparable to those of the USA and the UK, or even those of Switzerland.

At the institutional level, in the research universities while practices vary, on the whole there is insufficient recognition of the value of central leadership, planning, management and monitoring in achieving policy goals. It often appears that central executive capacity is weak *vis-à-vis* the faculties. There is inconsistent evidence of a performance economy within institutions, or a nuanced capacity for strategic adjustment of resources. There is little evidence that in either sector institutions consistently reward excellence in teaching (especially) and research according to agreed and transparent criteria. Decentralised allocations are more performance-related in some universities than others. Funding often tends to follow standardized formulae. At the central level at least some universities do not appear to have comprehensive data sets that can enable them to profile themselves in transparent fashion, and test faculty performance against targets.

Some interpret disciplinary autonomy as *sui generis* independence. Faculty independence is appropriate in determining the directions of research and scholarship. But autonomy should never be solely self-referencing and non-transparent. Teaching and research within academic units should always be coupled to tests of excellence and use. Nor should faculty activities be conducted in the absence of the centrally determined priorities, strategies and requirements of the institution. In Dutch research universities it is not always guaranteed that the faculties will work to fulfil institutional missions, achieve performance targets, optimise incomes and efficiencies, and secure identified developmental priorities. It is true that self-referencing operations can produce outstanding outcomes, but this is more so in very strong institutions where the tests of excellence are realistic, continuous and exacting, rather than merely ritualistic. One classic example of a strongly performing university coupled to a weak executive is the University of Cambridge in the UK. Given the demands of modernised administration and the intensely competitive character of global higher education such cases are exceptional; and even in such cases, when central and disciplinary strategies are not coordinated in optimum fashion results too are unlikely to be optimal.

It is not that research intensive university activities are conducted without reference to the external environment, more than in the present policy settings the connections between the external and internal dimensions are a hit and miss affair. For example, there seems to be insufficient awareness of comparative international benchmarks and performances, except at the level of fields of study and research groups. Likewise there is no necessary consistency between national and local mechanism and drivers. Reliance on Stream 1 for the bulk of research funding reduces the potential for the exercise of national strategic leadership in relation to research and academic development, the more so because by their nature the content of degree programmes are slow to change and teaching the costs are relatively fixed.

In both the research universities and the HBOs there seems to be insufficient awareness of the potential for diversifying and increasing revenues. Neither the drive to build commercial incomes, nor philanthropic incomes, is universally or strongly established (for more discussion see Chapter Four).

The HBOs would benefit from the development of a fuller range of instruments of steering such as performance monitoring, and strategic development funds distributed on a competitive basis. Compared to the research-intensive universities, the HBOs appear to have fewer professional staff attached to their executive boards. This reduces comparative steering capacity. Some HBOs also seem to reflect a more top down and bureaucratic culture with less capacity for initiative at the point of delivery of services. Perhaps enhancement of the capacity for autonomous action requires the emergence of an academically stronger leadership at the unit level of the HBOs but more could be done to nurture such an approach.

In both sectors innovations in the educational programme can take too long, inhibiting responsiveness. One research university administrator described to the review team an innovation cycle of 4-5 years duration. The HBOs do better in this regard: one HBO board member estimated the required time at 18 months. Both make an interesting comparison with the average time required to start a business in the Netherlands, which is 11 days (World Bank statistical data for 2004, *Netherlands data profile*).

Students have an important formal role in governance, particularly in institutions, but an under-developed role at national level. HBO students seem to have only a weak presence in national student organisation.

As noted, students have little effective authority in terms of resource power. There is notion of a student-centred market is formally acknowledged but in the context of near automatic entry systems and the absence of differential pricing this remains under-developed. Stream changing at the end of year one is not an empowering moment for students as it is driven by failure rather than success. The weakness of mature age student populations further weakens the potential drivers on the choice-making demand side. The provision of information to prospective students to guide choice of university and faculty is a stronger area (see Chapter Four).

3.4 Recommendations

The study team strongly recommends review of the mechanisms for policy coordination between the Department of Finance, the Department of Economic Affairs, and the Department of Education, Culture and Science, so as to ensure the more coherent alignment with national policy objectives and leadership, of programme administration in education and research.

It is further suggested that there be a review of existing OCW data collection, analysis and dissemination procedures in order to ensure more comprehensive coverage, and also greater national and international transparency of, and awareness of, the national system of higher education.

For any kind of binary line to be viable in the longer term it is necessary that both sectors are operating at a continuously advancing level of modernisation, with the capacity to shape both a national and international role, even while such roles may continue to differ between the sectors. If the HBOs are weakly integrated into national, European and global contexts, over time they are likely to become increasingly unattractive to local and foreign students, to potential faculty and to Dutch employers and the larger setting, so becoming increasingly destabilised and forced into measures designed to strengthen their profile regardless of the preferred national role or their real capacity.

The binary line should be rendered more dynamic over time, with freer variation across and between the sectors. More attention should be given to broadening student pathways between the two sectors (see Chapter Five) and to further increasing the institutional cooperation between them. However if the binary line is to be maintained then variations should take the form of collaborative arrangements and couplings of distinct units from each sector, rather than free-standing imitation and blending of functions. The basic research mission of the WOs, and their monopoly of research training in the form of research Masters and doctoral degrees, stands as the essential dividing line along which the binary system can be policed.

The occupational mission of the HBOs suggests that they should move more extensively into flexible short courses, continuing vocational education and associate degree programmes; professional Masters programmes on a comprehensive basis; and to augment their capacity in applied research, development and consultancy. These changes would strengthen the HBOs at the cutting edge of the industries and occupations they service, and improve their capacity to attract foreign students and collaborate with foreign universities. In the knowledge economy context, it is difficult to envisage reflexive advanced training that is not somewhere joined to an R&D capacity.

On the other hand the development of a broad HBO capacity in *basic* research would deplete resources needed for further building the research-intensive universities to global competitive levels of capacity and performance. In the absence of such an HBO research capacity it is impossible to justify the introduction of government funded research Masters and doctoral programmes – especially given that there are few HBO staff fully qualified to provide research degree supervision - or additional funds to support basic or strategic basic research in the HBOs. Without a significant capacity in basic research a university cannot be fully competitive in applied research and consultancy, but some such activities are within reach. The research role of the *lectoren* should be built in the form of teaching-led research, rather than trying to create research-led teaching as applies in the postgraduate programmes of research-intensive universities. The *lectoren* programme thereby would better contribute to the mission of the HBOs in professional education and while establishing a partial consultancy function serving SMEs.

Without creating the expectation of a level playing field in research funding, HBOs should be free to bid for competitive government research and consultancy funding, as AMK higher professional institutions are permitted to do in Finland. This is consistent with recent developments such as the *lectoren* programme and would ensure that as pockets of capacity develop in the HBOs, these become more fully accessible to the national innovation system. Inescapably, the augmentation of R&D capacity requires the employment of more doctorally trained staff in the HBOs. In the next decade it becomes possible to do this at scale, because a surfeit of PhDs in many disciplines, given the difficulty of obtaining faculty posts in the research intensive universities, coincides with the large number of impending retirements in the HBOs generated by the present age profile of HBO staff (further measures to develop research capacity in the HBOs are discussed in Chapter Seven).

In the research intensive universities the central research agencies could secure a greater strategic purchase on priorities if additional public support for research was channelled through Stream 2 (especially) and Stream 3 rather than Stream 1 funding - provided that Stream 2 was reworked to cover a greater proportion of the costs of research infrastructure so as to avoid the current disincentives to engage in Stream 2 activities, so better sustaining the foundation funding in Stream 1 (see Chapter Seven).

In relation to institutional diversity, consideration should be given to national policies designed to qualitatively strengthen selected research universities, possibly through additional funding for research infrastructure and programmes, and deregulation of academic remuneration to facilitate the appointment of high calibre foreign faculty and post-docs. Such a programme of fostering 'global universities' would need to be widely discussed within the Netherlands in order to facilitate the achievement of a threshold national consensus concerning the selection of the institutions.

Government could establish a project-based fund for institutional innovation in management and internal systems, subject to bidding. For example, institutions could submit proposals for funding for innovations in data collection systems and performance-based resource allocation.

At institutional level there is scope for substantial enhancement of the role of strategic funding in the hands of both central boards and of faculty deans and committees. It is noted that the Chang committee recommended the creation of a financial reserve at the level of the Board, for distribution on the basis of performance and of bids for innovations. Faculties and sub-faculty units, including research groups that raise additional private incomes should be rewarded by allocating them an enhanced proportion of public funding; provided that institutions continue to safeguard the resources of those disciplines with minor prospects of raising non-government income.

4. Resourcing Tertiary Education

4.1 Background

Tertiary education in the Netherlands is financed primarily by government support of institutions. Institutional support from public sources for 2006 is approximately EUR 5.3 billion. This represents an estimated 79% of total support, with approximately 21% provided by private sources such as tuition fees and private contributions. Based on 2003 data, the Netherlands is somewhat above the OECD average of 76% from public sources and below the average of 24% from private sources (OECD, 2006a). Separate government support of student financial aid of various types adds approximately EUR 1.7 billion to the overall effort.

The Netherlands' total financial support of tertiary education institutions is impressive by several measures. Comparing European Union countries on the basis of the 2006 figures, the Netherlands ranks third only behind Sweden and United Kingdom in expenditures per student, including research expenditures. Excluding research expenditures, the Netherlands ranks third only behind Denmark and Belgium. The amount of per student support in constant terms over the past eight years has not declined markedly, despite an overall increase in enrolment and an economic recession. (OCW, 2006c, Figures 24-27).

On the other hand, comparing per student expenditures relative to per capita GDP, the Netherlands ranks well below the OECD average and below several EU countries (OECD, 2006b, p. 122). Per student expenditures relative to GDP per capita are a measure of expenditure per student that has been standardized to national wealth. This shows that *relative to its national wealth*, and the size of its student population, the Netherlands is spending less on average than most other OECD nations.

Private support for institutions from tuition fee income and private contributions has been increasing slowly. A decade ago, private support made up approximately 19% compared to the current 21% (OECD, 2006a). Tuition fees, set at the national level (thereby eliminating competition among institutions), were EUR 1 496 for most students for 2005-06. Students who begin their studies too late, or take too long completing them, or take coursework unfunded by the government, must pay higher rates set by the institutions. The lack of a private university sector in the Netherlands' tertiary education configuration limits the potential of more market driven revenues from tuition fees.

In the research-intensive universities and in the HBOs between 1995 and 2006 there was almost no change in the proportion of total funding sourced from students (OCW, 2006c, pp. 51-52).

As noted in Chapter Three, over the past decade institutions have gained more autonomy, including ownership of their own campuses and capital facilities. Formula based, lump sum budgeting has replaced a more centralized, regulatory approach. Lump sum budgeting provides many advantages over alternative methods. It replaced a system in which excessive time and resources were devoted to regulatory compliance. The de-regulation of tertiary education has allowed institutions more flexibility and seems to be paying off with increased institutional cooperation and innovation. Institutions have merged with one another, worked together to create more programmes based on students' needs, and developed better working relationships in their respective regions, according to anecdotal evidence gathered in numerous interviews with institutional administrators.

The lump sum allocations are based on relatively simple formulas for distribution of financial support among both types of institutions in the binary system. Institutions' education budgets, exclusive of research, are made up of a base funding component, representing 37%, a results component calculated from the number of diplomas, representing 50%, and a component based on the number of first year students, representing 13%. For HBOs, total enrolment is used and dropouts are considered as well as students receiving diplomas. Another factor, to improve HBO efficiency, is added to the formula to encourage timely completion. If students take more than 4.5 years to graduate and dropouts remain more than 1.35 years, a proportionate factor of less than 1.0 is applied to the formula (Background Report, pp. 62-63). Research funding is added to the lump sum distributions for WOs and budget support for *lectoren* is added for HBOs, as discussed further in Chapter Seven.

Several years ago, public institutions were given both ownership and control of their own campuses and capital facilities. Capital expenditures and revenues are part of the lump sum budget, meaning that efficiencies and revenues in this category can be directed toward the operational needs of the institutions. This approach also encourages, at least theoretically, cooperative planning among institutions when constructing new facilities.

Institutions can use debt financing when necessary to pay for the facilities over the years of their useful lives.

In 2006 the Ministry of Education developed a bill – now suspended – proposing the implementation of student "learning entitlements." Under this proposal, when a student registered the national government would credit a payment directly to the enrolling institution, so that government support would follow students' enrolment choices more closely. Additionally, the proposed law envisioned moving towards a more differentiated system offering more choices in pricing, programmes and quality. If such a proposal were adopted, it would be a significant departure for the Netherlands in that competition between institutions might stimulate welcome changes such as improved teaching, programme innovations, changes in the relationships between costs and revenues, and additional discretionary revenues. There would also be difficulties with such an approach: for example, already strong institutions could take advantage of weaker ones without commensurate improvements. A differentiated system that entails student selection and pricing changes would also invite new questions about equity. (See more about equity in Chapter Five.) The student financial aid system would need to change to accommodate higher tuition fees. The Netherlands may need to look to other countries such as the United Kingdom for new or additional student finance models. All of these possibilities are likely to stimulate debate on the mechanisms and limits of differentiation. The possibility of selection 'at the gate' or point of entry is itself a big shift in policy. These matters may be reconsidered by the new government that has been formed in 2007.

Grants to students (which, unlike loans, do not have to be paid back provided the student graduates in time) totalled EUR 786.2 million in 2004. A basic grant is provided to all students, and there is a supplementary grant related to parental income for those of lesser means. Since 2000, the duration of grants has been limited to the normal number of years it takes to complete the course. If students are still studying at the end of that time they must find alternative finance (Background Report, p. 20). One way is to take a loan from the government. Students can take a loan of up to EUR 800 per month, for three years after the grant period. During this time they receive the public transportation allowance as a grant. A public transportation allowance provides students an additional 298 million Euro benefit, and loans to students add another EUR 597 million. In 2003 25.9% of all public expenditure on tertiary education in the Netherlands was in the form of financial aid to students. This was the 6th highest level among OECD nations and compared with an OECD average of 16.6% (OECD, 2006a, p. 242). These comparatively generous student aid programmes represent significant tax spending transfers independent of family income (and as such, they favour middle class families). At the same time students from poorer backgrounds receive the additional supplementary grant. At present 30% of students receive the supplementary grant and a total of 43% of all grants (basic, supplementary and public transportation) go to those students.

Loans are not considered outlays in the national budget inasmuch as they provide future revenue for the government. Student loans are handled through the government so as to avoid excessive student loan subsidies to banks. Loans provide relatively generous repayment terms, including a grace period of two years before repayment begins, forbearances for low earnings, and 15-year loan terms after which further repayments are cancelled. The initial loan default rate of approximately 10% is reduced further by systematic collection efforts. From 2007 a new law for student financial aid will be implemented, with loans to cover college fees - an additional loan the size of the tuition fee that the student has to pay will be available during the grant and the loan period. Repayment terms for the loans will remain unchanged, including the option for students to choose income contingent repayment.

Vocational programmes funded by employer fees add substantially to government support of tertiary education. Although not all programmes of a 2.8 billion Euro annual fee-based fund are for the education of students, the employers' payments make a major contribution to the overall effort.

Allowing students to use their government student financial aid at such institutions leverages the resources of private, accredited tertiary institutions. There is some interest among both private institutions and the government in increasing the role of the private education sector in reaching the country's tertiary education goals, but lacking a tradition of private institutions there is no strong push to do so.

Faculty resources have been strength of Dutch tertiary education for decades. But a very low percentage of academic faculty in the HBOs have PhDs, while the number of PhDs being prepared for academic careers, particularly in science and technology disciplines, is low (see also Chapter Seven). The age of faculty is a growing concern given the need for replacements. This is a particular problem in the HBOs given their age structure. In the HBOs in 2003, 46.3% of faculty were aged 50 years or more (OCW, 2006b, p. 85). Age-related problems in the universities are not as severe but to the extent that there are shortages of staff for the universities this will worsen the pressures on the HBOs and make it more difficult for them to lift the proportion of staff with PhDs. Therefore in 2007 staff in the HBOs will be encouraged to begin PhDs studies. From 2008 onwards the ministry will set aside EUR 10 million a year for this purpose; in 2007 EUR 6 million is available. Institutions will become more reliant on foreign migrants and offshore recruitment emphasising the need to improve the global drawing power of the system (for more discussion of this aspect see Chapter Nine). Contributing to the problem of staffing is the current lack of incentives for young people who may be contemplating faculty careers. This conceivably could be dealt with in the new law, discussed above.

Women are not represented proportionately either in scientific research or in faculty positions in general, especially at higher ranks. 'The Netherlands ranks quite low in Europe for historical and cultural reasons'. In 2004 only 9.4% of professors in the Netherlands were female compared to 21.2% in Finland, 16.1% in France, 16.1% in Sweden and 15.9% in the UK. Some progress is being made, with the ratio in the Netherlands lifting to 9.9% in 2005. At senior lecturer level 15.7% were women. Among doctoral candidates in 2005, 41.5% were women (Stichting de Beauvoir, 2006).

In 2004 the overall Netherlands ratio of students to tertiary teaching staff of 13.6 students per equivalent full-time faculty was lower than the OECD average of 15.5, though the Netherlands ratio was not especially low in the European context (OECD, 2006a, p. 371).

4.2 Strengths

As the above account suggests, Dutch higher education has a number of resourcing strengths. Expenditure per student is relatively high compared to other nations in the EU. Student financial aid programmes are generous, being funded at approximately EUR 1.7 billion for 2006 (a figure that also includes subsidies to parents of low-income students 12 and above, *i.e.* in secondary education).

The provision of information to facilitate student choice is advancing. The website *studiekeuze123* looks promising. Using this, students can compare bachelor- and master-level studies in all higher education institutions. It is comparable to the German CHE system, though at the time of finalising this review report was more extensive than CHE in the area of labour market-related data and weaker in relation to research and internationalisation. From January 2007 forward, *studiekeuze123* is available in English, providing wider international access to study information.

Lump sum budgeting provides autonomy and flexibility. It is clearly superior to those national funding systems where detailed expenditures are prescribed from the centre. In addition the funding procedures for capital facilities encourage cooperation and efficiencies among institutions.

The private sector supplements public effort in several ways. Employers add vocational funding to the mix. Local and foreign students pay tuition fees, at differing rates appropriate to their differing lifetime tax relationships with government. Private institutions are utilised by allowing students to use their government student financial aid at such institutions.

4.3 Weaknesses

Several of the resourcing strengths listed above can be interpreted differently using other measures, as some of the strengths carry with them inherent weaknesses. The Netherlands' financial support of tertiary education as a share of gross domestic product is not as strong as it is per student support, and some of the budget and finance procedures have downsides.

Private funding support, from tuition fees and private contributions, is only slightly below average overall but noteworthy for certain practices and attitudes that depart from the norm. Tuition fees may be much higher for students over the age of thirty and for students taking unsubsidized courses of study, which may raise additional revenues but which also suppresses participation.[5] Additionally, there is a longstanding view strongly held among the Dutch that because they pay relatively high taxes, tertiary education, including research, should rely on government financing. This limits financing possibilities on the revenue side of budgets.

The move toward lump sum, formula budgeting, driven increasingly by student choices and implemented without a budget request and negotiation process, has left many institutions without a sense of what the government wants or needs from them. As noted in Chapter Three, guidance and communication from the ministries are weak, whether via funding mechanisms or other means. The question of what the government wants for its funding support is fundamental to the whole endeavour, yet there is no clear reasoning behind any particular level of funding other than the most general social, economic, and tax equity rationales. This leaves tertiary education funding vulnerable to competing claims with more urgent messages (global warming and low country flooding, for one), and threatens erosion of the tertiary education system to the point that it may become shabby over time.

---

[5] To be publicly subsidized, a course of study must be taken in an accredited programme at recognised institution. A course taken at an unaccredited programme at an *angewezen* institution, or in a HBO master's programme that has not been authorized for public subsidy, is not publicly subsidised.

Many institutions themselves do not fully utilise the possibilities available to them under lump sum budgeting. Not surprisingly, the basic government formula is often used for internal allocations among departments and other entities, but rarely do institutions have offices of institutional research, strategic plans, and budgeting processes to innovate and differentiate on their own. Following student demand too closely at the institutional level can lead to self-defeating cycles in neither the institutions' nor the country's interest. For example, the current lack of student interest in certain science and technology fields can lead to departmental cut-backs, loss of staff and quality, and subsequently less demand, despite the acknowledged need for higher quality programmes and more graduates in these fields.

Relying on student learning entitlements so that funding follows student choice has its limitations. In the Netherlands, institutions have traditionally been undifferentiated in terms of quality and many offer similar programmes and degrees. Many if not most students therefore make choices based on geography or friendships or other personal reasons.

Several institutions have ambitious and innovative ideas for programmes to increase participation among underserved populations, to increase linkages with secondary schools, to create residential campuses, to offer higher quality programmes at commensurately higher prices, to articulate programmes between institutions, to work with particular businesses and industries, and other noteworthy efforts. Despite lump sum budgeting and fewer regulations, these innovations may not be undertaken without higher approval from the government either through special grants and dispensations or through expressly authorised pilot and demonstration programmes.

The current pilot and demonstration projects are few, unsystematic, and of questionable value as experiments from which to make firm inferences about the effects of policies. Findings from current projects will be only anecdotal and site-specific. There are no built in research and evaluation components so as to be able to generalize for purposes of broader implementations.

Staffing in tertiary education institutions has not received adequate policy attention. This might be because human resources policy is the autonomous responsibility of the institutions; though the ministry subsidizes programmes for specific target groups like outstanding female and *allochtone* (foreign Dutch national) researchers (Aspasia and Mozaïek). The HBOs lack a fully-fledged academic capacity, yet the opportunity to address this may pass if tendencies to shortage take hold across both sectors. As noted, a growing portion of faculty is nearing retirement age and replacement will be difficult. There are few incentives exist to recruit and retain outstanding faculty.

Capital needs at institutions will increasingly compete with operational needs as current facilities grow older and new plant and equipment are required. Institutions may have more assets on their books by virtue of owning their own campuses, but such assets cannot easily be converted into revenues to meet new capital or operational needs.

Student financial aid is available to all and is not focused primarily on the financially needy. Basic grant and transportation subsidy expenditures for students who doubtless will be participating in tertiary education inevitably compete with financial support for students whose participation depends on adequate aid, and with adequate financial support for outstanding teaching and research at institutions.

Despite a student loan programme with generous repayment conditions, many students choose to work rather than take advantage of such loans. The fact that so many students feel they have time to work may reflect a lack of demanding studies. Interviews with students and faculty suggest that students would welcome greater academic challenges. For some students who do not qualify for low tuition fees at public and private institutions, current loan limits are inadequate. The new law improves this situation.

In vocational education, some employer groups are dissatisfied with public education programmes and prefer students who are trained through the programmes of the 2.8 billion Euro fund provided by employers. This suggests duplication of effort and programme inefficiencies that potentially could be reduced by better coordination between public education and industry.

Although the Netherlands makes good use of its private, accredited tertiary education institutions by permitting students to use government grants and loans at such institutions, the government lacks systematically collected information about these students' ages, ethnicities, incomes, reasons for enrolling, and other important characteristics. Without this information, resourcing policy options cannot be well informed about a significant sector of the country's overall tertiary education efforts.

4.4 Recommendations

If the Netherlands is to be a top leader of Europe's knowledge-based economies, it must invest commensurately in a tertiary education system that produces and disseminates such knowledge. This will require additional resources devoted to tertiary education as a share of GDP, to match other European leaders.

The needs of the tertiary education system to which additional resources could wisely be applied include widening participation, improving faculty qualifications at HBOs, seeking and retaining outstanding faculty at all levels, investing in research and development, and other needs as identified in more detail in other sections of this report. The recommendations that follow concern the means by which such needs might be financed.

The existing system, which has many areas of strength, probably cannot be radically overhauled, because it has evolved out of Dutch tradition and modified within the limits of political feasibility. But simply adding more resources into current distribution patterns may not get the best results, in view of the aforementioned weaknesses inherent in the existing system.

Consequently, the Netherlands should consider adding a separate channel of funding that is different from the current distributions, in order to stimulate new initiatives on both the expenditure and revenue sides of tertiary education budgets. Many institutions are ready to address national needs by differentiating themselves in terms of new programmes and programme quality, new responses to industry needs, targeting populations including minorities and adult learners, international education, student selection, and price differentiation. Rewarding these initiatives financially would move them ahead more quickly and provide additional incentives for more efforts.

The mechanisms for such incentives could be adjustments to current formula-funding coefficients, matching fund programmes, or competitions at the national level to address government identified concerns (which would simultaneously address the current problem of 'What does the government want?').

Similarly, in research funding the proportion of support provided in the form of performance-related monies and strategic initiative should be increased relative to basic research support. These issues are discussed more fully in Chapter Three and especially in Chapter Seven.

The amounts involved in a new channel of funding may not be as important as establishing processes by which additional funds can be wisely invested. New initiatives should be financed only if they are clearly tied to national goals and implemented in such a way that they can be evaluated.

The revenue side of the budget offers opportunities to increase resources by experimenting with student selection and price differentiation. In our meetings we were told that some students want greater academic challenges, shorter degree completion times, and more stimulating learning experiences and are willing to pay higher tuition fees for them. Some institutions have good relationships with industry that could lead to greater private contributions to the institutions' unrestricted funds. Although it has not been part of the modern Dutch higher education tradition to seek revenues from differentiated tuition rates and from private fund raising, encouraging long term experimentation with increasing revenues from sources that benefit from strong tertiary education would help answer questions of where revenues can and should come from if the Netherlands is to be a top leader among European knowledge-based economies. The experience of the United Kingdom should be of particular interest in diversifying revenue sources for tertiary education.

Private, accredited institutions should not be excluded from participation in incentive funding channels where they may have an important function because they serve a particular population, or have special ties to an industry branch, or provide healthy competition for excellence and cost with public institutions.

Government ministries that deal with tertiary education resourcing should be strengthened in terms of data collection, analysis, evaluation, policy development, and policy implementation.

5. *Access and Equity*

5.1 Background

In the Netherlands, there are 534 600 students enrolled in public tertiary education institutions (2004) and an estimated 70 000 students in private, accredited institutions. Enrolments have been increasing in recent years both in numbers of students and percentages of the overall population (OCW, 2006b, Fig. 2.11, Fig. 2.13; OCW, 2005, Fig. 17). Because of differences in educational systems and definitions, it is difficult to rank countries on participation indicators, but the Netherlands appears to compare competitively with Sweden, Finland, Denmark, the United Kingdom, Canada, and the United States on many participation measures (CHEPS, 2005).

The nation aspires to have a tertiary education participation rate of 50% of its population by 2010, and it has outlined strategies to meet the goal (OCW, 2004b, p. 24; CHEPS, 2005, pp. 26-27). Although there are different ways of calculating participation rates, by most measures the Netherlands is currently a few percentage points short of its goal. Projections based on current participation policies indicate that the goal may be reached within a decade but perhaps not by the target date. The strategy to achieve the target rate has three components: increasing recruitment from underrepresented groups, increasing recruitment from upper secondary vocational graduates, and increasing completion rates.

Current policy focuses attention on full-time participation among the traditional 18-30 age group. Students who obtain certain secondary school qualifications must be accepted into Netherlands' public tertiary education institutions. A six-year university preparatory education (VWO) qualifies for admittance to an academic university (WO) or to a higher professional education institution (HBO); a five-year general secondary education (HAVO) qualifies for admittance to an HBO, as does a senior four-year, level 4 vocational education (MBO). HBO students can enter university programmes with their *propaedeuse* diploma from an HBO, and they can enter a WO master's programme with their HBO bachelor degree. In practice this route may be difficult, owing to the necessity of HBO students taking bridging programmes that may not be funded, or lack of transparency in admission requirements. All public institutions may grant admission by testing. The Open University has no entrance requirements.

Several student equity issues confront the Netherlands. Completion rates for non-western immigrant populations remain lower than for other populations. Full-time students who complete their degrees quickly are favoured over part-time students. Family income seems to be an important determinant of tertiary education participation. Students above age thirty do not receive the same financial support as traditional age college students, detracting from the Netherlands' lifelong learning effort. The enrolment percentage of the age 30-39 population is only 2.9, compared to an OECD average of 5.6, and of the age 40 and over population it is only 0.8, compared to an OECD average of 1.6 (OECD, 2006a, C1).

Some of the equity issues arising in tertiary education may be the result of the selection and sorting that goes on in primary and secondary schools, plus the difficulty of moving between streams. Although the OECD team did not review primary and secondary education procedures, the team heard this explanation frequently from tertiary educators. Mobility between the VMBO stream and the HAVO stream - which is a key element if the expectations of lower achieving students, their families and their teachers are to remain open, so that the negative potential of early streaming to create social segmentation is minimised – appears to have fluctuated in recent years. It dropped to a low level after system restructuring before returning close to previous levels. The review team detected little concern about this issue during the process of consultation. Much later, there is provision for MBO graduates to move to the HBOs, and HBO graduates to enter research-intensive universities (WOs). However, students wanting to follow these routes are restricted in their potential areas of study by their prior learning. 'By the time we see them many selection moments have passed', as one HBO executive said to the review team. Again, the review team detected little concern about rates of mobility or transfer. On the other hand, there is encouraging evidence that more students are moving between streams at the tertiary level. Students moving from HBO to WO totalled approximately 4 500 in 2000, but 6 700 students followed that pathway in 2004 (OCW, 2006b, p. 19).

Participation by non-western minorities is a significant issue in the Netherlands as in other European countries. On the positive side, it should be noted that total participation is increasing, both in research-intensive universities and HBOs (OCW, 2006b, p. 18). Several efforts are underway at both the government and institutional level to increase it further (Country Background Report, p. 54). The government has encouraged tertiary education institutions to develop plans to increase enrolments of ethnic populations, encouraged HBOs and upper secondary vocational schools (MBOs) to reach agreement on linkages, and encouraged all institutions to improve completion rates. In 2004 there was an intake of 7 748 non-Western non-native Dutch students into the HBOs representing 13.4% of the intake. The corresponding figures for the research intensive universities were 2 242 and 8.2% (OCW, 2006b, p. 99).

Nevertheless, the relative participation and completion of non-western students remains an issue. Participation growth has indeed moved up in step with the growth in the overall tertiary population (Background Report, p. 50), but completion is still behind (OCW, 2005, Fig. 24). As noted in Chapter Three, some large Dutch cities will be majority minority in a few years.

The OECD's Programme for International Student Assessment singles out the Netherlands among several countries where immigrant populations are markedly less well prepared than native students in subjects such as reading, mathematics, and science (OECD, 2006c, p.8).

Further, although non-western students are enrolling in greater numbers in the Dutch tertiary education system, their success rates in graduating are markedly lower than that of the native Dutch. In the HBOs, for the cohort beginning in 2000, the gap after five years was 20 percentage points. At the research-intensive universities it was 10 percentage points. The trend in the gaps seems steady, meaning that progress, if any, is slow. It is noteworthy, however, that fewer non-western minorities are leaving their studies. For example, at the research-intensive universities, the proportion of non-western students who leave after five years without awards has fallen from 20% to 15% over the past six cohorts. These persistence trends are encouraging (Centraal Bureau voor de Statistiek, Voorburg/Heerlen 2006-6-20).

Although the overall participation goal has been set, where students from the non-western populations fit in is unclear. The government provides only minor programmes in this area (Background Report, p. 54). There appears to be considerable complacency among the Dutch about raising the participation rates of the non-western populations. The only organisation that made a strong point of raising this issue with the review team was HBO-raad. The matter was addressed at some length in the report *Bridging the Gap Between Theory and Practice*, prepared by an international panel (NVAO, 2005). That report also remarked on the fact that 'the lack of permeability in Dutch higher education is apparently ... well accepted by stakeholders' (pp. 47-48), referring to the difficulties faced by students when they attempt to move from the segment to which they have been assigned.

On several occasions the OECD review team asked various groups of faculty, administrators, students, government officials, business organisations, researchers, and others to describe their vision of what Dutch tertiary education should look like within the next ten years. No respondents mentioned increasing the participation of non-western populations. On a more positive note, the review team visited a few institutions where there was genuine enthusiasm for increasing non-western participation. At the *Haagse Hogeschool*, an HBO, administrators showed the review team how it had adapted techniques borrowed from TRIO and GEAR-UP programmes in the United States to achieve impressive successes.

5.2 Strengths

The Netherlands has a strong sense of equity for participants in tertiary education. Tuition fees are set low at public institutions for students beginning by age 30 years, regardless of income. Substantial basic grants and subsidised public transportation are likewise available to all. For students from higher income families, this is considered equitable in view of higher taxes paid. For the lower income student, needs-based grants supplement the basic grants. Student loans may be written off for students with low subsequent incomes. Government grants and loans can be used at private, accredited institutions.

As noted, participation rates are slowly rising. The 50% goal is being pursued, though participation targets are less important and urgent in the Netherlands than in some other nations.

Within the overall trend, participation by non-western minorities is increasing in both the research-intensive universities and the HBOs (though not their share of total enrolments). Their completion rates are also improving.

Participation by women has been substantially improved and parity has been achieved on many measures. The percentage of women in doctoral programmes is still low but has increased from 18% in 1990 to 41% in the most recent compilations (Background Report, p. 50). Continued progress on this measure is essential if the percentage of women in university faculties is to increase.

Of the dropouts from HBOs, a majority eventually succeeds in degree completion at either the same or another institution (OCW, 2006b, p. 82).

The Open University provides distance education for those who need or prefer this form of educational delivery. Associate degrees are being added to the options available in tertiary education, and this will attract additional participation.

5.3 Weaknesses

The Netherlands may achieve its 50% participation target in the next few years (OCW, 2005, Fig. 18) but it may take somewhat longer than planned and prospects for yet wider participation are limited.

In part this is because students are tracked away from tertiary education paths at age twelve, when many have not yet had the time to show the ability or inclination to succeed at the higher level. Tracking students away at an early age makes it difficult for them to change curricula in secondary school.

Another reason why national improvements in participation are difficult to achieve is that subsidies cut out for students commencing after the age of 30 years. Lifelong learners are not given the same financial considerations as those in their teens and twenties to pursue or continue tertiary education. It is not surprising that, as shown above, the Netherlands' rate of enrolment beyond age 30 is roughly half of the OECD average. This spells trouble for a country that aspires to be a leader in a knowledge-based world, as knowledge bases are in continual change and leading countries are likely to be those that provide lifelong tertiary education to their populations.

The principle of equity that characterizes the approach to tertiary education is not synonymous with equality of opportunity. For those who have the right preparation, are the right age, and have the right kind of family situation, there are abundant opportunities within the tertiary education system of the Netherlands. But potential students from underserved groups who lack necessary language skills, educational preparation, or have no family members to support them, have more difficulty entering the system. The secondary school tracking system, as it currently exists, may be an impediment to achieving greater equity.

To the extent that the populations that are disproportionately excluded from higher education have considerable numbers of talented people who can contribute to the Dutch knowledge-based economy, the nation's human resources are not being well exploited. The completion rates in higher education of non-western groups are clearly below average. Not enough is being done about this.

There are few data collected on income by ethnicity in tertiary education, so it is difficult to sort out whether participation gaps may be related to ethnicity or to income. This hinders analysis of equity issues and makes initiatives to improve equity difficult to evaluate. Equity issues in terms of completion are largely unidentified because data by ethnicity and income are likewise not compiled except for the occasional research study. Data on the ethnic composition of faculty are also lacking (Background Report, p. 56).

Little policy consideration is given to special incentives to encourage students to study in areas that are important to the country. There are low enrolments of students in secondary education, but scholarships, loan forgiveness programmes, and similar incentives are not among the Netherlands' approaches for addressing these needs. In areas where there are too many students, such as pharmacy and certain biological sciences, *numerus fixus* limits have been imposed. Selective student admission into popular or high quality programmes is not yet widely practiced. However, the exertion of greater control over selection (which was raised by the Chang committee) is a desirable reform that could be used to address a number of policy goals.

Completion may be difficult for students who do not stay on specified tracks that are subsidised. To the extent that institutions wish to recover costs, they must charge higher tuition for certain unfunded programmes, including research masters degrees at the HBOs, for students who have exceeded age limits, and students who attend private institutions which charge higher tuition. The government grant and loan system does not recognize the greater financial needs of such students. The expectation that businesses or family members or other sources should pay for their costs must lessen overall participation to some extent. The new law on student grants and loans improves this situation. It provides for additional loans for fees to a maximum of five times the publicly set fee.

5.4 Recommendations

Because the Netherlands already has considerable success in many aspects of tertiary education participation, and continued improvements are underway, there seems to be no need to make fundamental changes to an already functioning system. Nevertheless, there is a need to follow through with more clearly defined and purposeful measures to implement the strategy that has been outlined for increasing participation.

The main area where change is needed is not so much at the tertiary level as the secondary level. The nation's failure to increase the number of students prepared for tertiary education is a serious problem. A related problem is the lack of students prepared at the secondary level for tertiary studies in science and technology fields. These students have a special leadership role in a knowledge-based economy.

The former problem could be addressed by providing more opportunities in secondary schools for children and their families to prepare for tertiary education, for example by lowering the barriers between the career and tertiary education tracks. In the end, postponement of the present early selection regime seems inevitable, although this is a major change in the way Dutch society thinks of itself.

Teacher training institutions could address the latter problem advantageously. Recruiting more students into secondary teaching and improving the quality of the academic preparation of secondary teachers are two steps that government and institutions could be taking more aggressively. Good academic preparation of teachers in the sciences and technology is important so that well-qualified teachers can inspire more secondary students to pursue studies in these fields. This needs to be done regardless of labour market conditions at any given time, or current economic sector strengths or weaknesses in the national economy. Science and technology graduates are well prepared for career contributions in many areas, and are valuable resources in a country whatever its economic aspirations and strategies.

There is considerable anecdotal information that suggests recruiting more secondary teachers from underserved minority groups would also raise tertiary education participation in these communities. Many individuals, both in the academic institutions and among minorities, report that teachers coming from outside these communities are too inclined to track non-western minority children away from tertiary education. An additional concern expressed to the OECD team was that secondary school funding rewards schools that prepare students for tertiary education, making the situation more difficult for schools where non-western students are tracked away.

Just as the Netherlands seems not to be focusing on increasing the numbers of students being prepared for tertiary education, the country also makes only limited efforts to encourage lifetime leaning. Students who do not begin their degree programmes before age thirty lose both institutional and student aid subsidies. The experiences of other countries indicate that the Netherlands could raise its participation rate by being more accommodating to older learners. This could also pay dividends in an improved capacity for work force related upgrading and refresher courses.

Focusing more attention on pre-18 and post-30 populations would require additional resources, but the Netherlands could revise its current approach to equity in order to expand opportunity to these groups. The basic grant could be converted from non-need to need-based, essentially reducing subsidies to those whose participation is not dependent on student aid. The savings could be redirected into programmes that focus on the currently underserved, especially those younger and older than the traditional college-aged. Alternatively, the Netherlands could allow the basic grant to exist at current levels without increase, and place new monies into programmes that are better designed to increase participation. This would provide a shift in resources over time in real terms rather than being an abrupt change.

6. Labour Markets and Tertiary Education

6.1 Introduction

The Netherlands has an educational system that, viewed in international perspective, is strongly oriented towards employer engagement and working life. At the secondary level, a large proportion of students study in vocational programmes, while at the tertiary level perhaps the largest share of students in any OECD country study in professionally oriented institutions of higher education, *hogescholen*. Tertiary education policies establish a national policy framework for *hogescholen* that is strongly oriented towards employer engagement. Additionally, the tertiary system is one in which demand-driven, *i.e.* in which the number of study places and courses of study offered are adapted to student choices.[6] Thus, students can respond to labour market signals - unemployment and wages associated with alternative occupations - and to adapt their study choices accordingly.

The Netherlands labour market offers graduates of tertiary education comparatively modest returns on their investment. One recent estimate of the *average* rate of return to tertiary education suggests that it is about 6.95% – well below the EU-14 average rate of 8.78%, and far below that of economies such as Germany (9.13), Finland (9.98), and the UK (12.25) (Fuente and Jimeno, 2005).[7] Closer analysis of the Netherlands case suggests that comparatively modest returns are not due to the high costs of tertiary study (direct costs or opportunity costs), but rather the comparatively modest impact that tertiary qualifications have in the Netherlands - relative to upper secondary qualifications - with respect to the

---

[6] Unlike other demand-driven systems, such as the UK or US, the Netherlands (like Flanders) has a system in which selection *at the point of entry* is not used. Rather, students have the right to study on the course and at the institution of their choice - subject to quotas or *numerus fixus* in some study fields. This aspect of the system is taken up elsewhere in the report.

[7] An earlier review of the literature on returns to education in the Netherlands (Hartog *et al.*, 1999) identified a range of estimates from 3 to 8.6 percent.

probability of unemployment and wages. The private rate of return to schooling for those who graduate from a HBO programme is, on average, significantly smaller than that of university graduate: an unpublished 2001 study by the CPB estimated of the private rate of return for an HBO degree to be approximately half that of a university degree (5.5%, as opposed to 10%) (Canton, 2001).

Social partners, researchers, and public officials have raised questions about the tertiary system's adequacy in addressing labour market needs. There have been frequently voiced concerns that the nation's tertiary education system is not producing a sufficient number of science and technology graduates, and thus failing to nurture and sustain high technology growth in the Dutch economy. The connection between employers and HBO sector - while often quite cooperative at a local level - has been marked by marked by conflict at the level of national policy. And, the review team itself is not fully confident that the needs of learners are fully being met by either sector in the binary system.

6.2 Labour Market Connections - Strengths

The structure of Netherlands secondary and tertiary education is organised with an unusually strong orientation towards working life. In upper secondary education 69.1% of students are enrolled in vocational programmes of study, a share half again greater than the OECD average (45.4%). At the level of tertiary study, about two-thirds of undergraduate students are enrolled in *hogescholen*. These institutions offer *hoger beroepsonderwijs (HBO)*, or higher professional education, the aim of which is to prepare students for working life. This percentage is far higher that of other binary systems within the OECD, including Finland (in which 47% of undergraduate students are enrolled at AMK institutions), or the tertiary systems of Switzerland (29%), Germany (25%), or Austria (9%).

Dutch *hogescholen* are linked to working life and employers through pedagogy and instructional staff; through employer participation in the supervisory boards of HBO institutions; and in advisory relationships with between employers and *hogescholen* that extend from the development of programmes to their quality assurance. All HBO courses are to have one or more traineeship, thus students experience part of their learning in a work-based setting. *Hogescholen* instructors are professionals drawn for working life. Ideally, their instructors remain professionally engaged throughout their teaching careers, providing a bridge between working life and classroom instruction. Local employers often sit in the governing bodies of *hogescholen*, and national sectoral organisations may be consulted in the development of study domain competencies (*domeincompetenties*)[8] and *opleidingskwalificaties*. Quality assessment panels are required to have employers from the related field of work as panel participants. Student labour market outcomes are monitored by the *arbeidsmarkt monitor* (labour market monitor), HBO-Labour market monitor, an HBO-Council publication that has since 1993 monitored the employment and wages of tertiary HBO graduates (ECABO, 2006). Additionally, the Ministry of Education publishes the *Studentenmonitor (www.studentenmonitor.nl)*, which has since 2000 surveyed student income, student backgrounds, and other topics.[9]

The relationship between the WO (university) sector and working life is very different to that of the HBO sector. There are 13 publicly funded research universities in the Netherlands offering *wetenschappelijk onderwijs*, or scientific education.[10] However, four of these thirteen universities are not traditional research universities with Humboldtian roots; rather, three are technical universities (Delft, Eindhoven, and Twente), while another is a university in the domain of agriculture and natural environment (Wageningen). Based upon visits to the first of these institutions - and secondary materials concerning the others - it appears to us that they have robust connections to employers and working life. Additionally, we must acknowledge that even research universities with a strongly theoretical and research-led orientation offer study programmes are in fact strongly oriented towards working life – including programmes in traditionally vocational study fields, such as architecture, law, and medicine.

6.3 Weaknesses

Though the national policy framework appears in many respects to provide a strong foundation for labour market engagement, concerns have often been raised that the tertiary system has a key labour market failure-that if fails to produce sufficient numbers of tertiary graduates in science and engineering, or *beta-techniek* students. Viewed in comparison to other OECD countries the Netherlands does have a small share of science and engineering graduates, and a declining share, as well. In the 1970's about 25% of university graduates were in science and engineering fields, while three decades later this level had fallen to about 18%. By way of contrast,

---

[8] Study domain competencies may be found at: http://www.hbo-raad.nl/?id=155

[9] www.studentmonitor.nl

[10] There are also 10 recognised institutions of *wetenschappelijk onderwijs* that are not funded by the state.

OECD REVIEWS OF TERTIARY EDUCATION – NETHERLANDS – ISBN 978-92-64-03925-4 – © OECD 2008

German (31.2), Finland (31.2), and France (29.0) all had a much higher share of science and engineering students among their tertiary graduates.

A very careful review of the available labour market evidence shows no evidence of a shortage of science and engineering graduates relative to labour market demand. As the Netherlands Bureau for Economic Policy Analysis (CPB) notes in *Scarcity of Science and Engineering Graduates in the Netherlands* (CPB, 2005), tight labour markets are characterised by high wages, high labour force participation rates, low unemployment, long working hours, and high vacancy rates.[11] A review of labour market data reveals that the opposite is the case - that the labour market position of science and engineering graduates relative to other tertiary education graduates has been deteriorating. The wage premium of science and engineering graduates from HBO and university programmes relative to that of all other graduates - and compared to a comparison group of economics graduates - has deteriorated since the early to mid-1990s.

CPB analysts speculate that this might be due, in part, to the internationalisation of research and development activities, and to the internationalisation of the labour market for science and engineering graduates. Internationalisation leads firms to locate R&D in countries having a comparative advantage to the Netherlands, and provides Dutch firms with access to an international of science and engineering graduates. Both developments have the effect of bring wages for Dutch science and engineering graduates into line with the international market for science and engineering workers - *i.e.* at a wage that may be lower than that of competing Dutch labour markets.[12]

As compared to other systems of tertiary education, the Netherlands system is marked by a relatively low degree of differentiation – within its university system, and within its *hogescholen* sector. Though there are 67 publicly funded tertiary education institutions in the Netherlands,[13] students are chiefly made an offer of two different kinds of education, with very little in the way of differentiation with respect to institutional culture and mission, pedagogy, the pacing and flexibility of study, pricing, and peer characteristics within each sector.

---

[11] Similar results for 1985-1996 are provided by Groot and Plug (1999).

[12] SEO, The Foundation for Economic Research of the University of Amsterdam, is also undertaking a study of wages among science and engineering graduates in the Netherlands.

[13] And an additional 73 recognised institutions of tertiary education that are not state funded.

Predictably, students in the Netherlands frequently attend a tertiary education institution near the place of residence - a sensible decision in a system in which institutions are not seen to differ significantly. The fact that students travel greater distances (or relocate) to study at Wageningen University and Maastricht University - two institutions that are distinctive by virtue of their study programmes and pedagogy, respectively - suggests that Dutch students are not averse to relocation.

University institutions (providing *wetenschappelijk onderwijs*) may want to establish a distinctive profile or niche, but they have little scope to do so within the existing framework of national policy - in which student selection and price differentiation are not possible.

There are examples of striking departures from the norm in the university sector - in which universities have experimented with a shift away from what critics have described as 'factory-style' university education, and towards a tutorial or seminar model of education - including University College Utrecht, University College Maastricht, and Roosevelt Academy. However, these have been permitted a very limited and precarious scope of development, and enrol only a trace of the overall university student population. There may be too little price differentiation possible under the current policy framework to permit this to be a widespread and sustainable model of education.

Alternatively, universities may wish to alter their balance of graduate and undergraduate study towards the former, so as to better support an international research profile, but in a system in which undergraduate student numbers carrying substantial funding implications, and cannot easily be replaced by other revenue streams, this is difficult.

Most often, critics of the national policy framework note, non-selection and price uniformity drive university institutions to expand student numbers across a wide range of course offerings. Many of these newer courses, they note, do not have the *wetenschappelijk* foundation of traditional academic disciplines – but provide instead an interdisciplinary education that may be topical, but not strongly oriented toward working life and the development of professional skills.

With respect to the HBO sector, too, there is frustration about insufficient diversification. Seen from the vantage point of HBO institutions and their sectoral organisation (the *HBO-Raad*) *hogescholen* should be given wider opportunities to develop professional master-level education, and to enhance their research capacities.

Employer associations – both those representing both large firms and those representing small and medium-sized enterprises - took the opposite view, arguing that HBO institutions should take on neither expanded graduate education nor wider research responsibilities. Rather, they express a desire to see HBO institutions offer a much wider range of study options - such as blended work and learning provided on a part-time basis. By international standards the HBO sector offers very little of its provision on a part-time or dual basis (15 and 1%, respectively), which fits poorly with its mission of providing *hoger beroepsonderwijs* to a diverse population of learners. Additionally, their preference is that the HBO sector focuses on the initiation of short-cycle (two-year) degree that would provide additional workers with a set of intermediate qualifications now lacking in the Netherlands education and training system.

In response to persistent concerns about a lack of differentiation, policymakers have authorised very limited initiatives permitting pilot programmes of differentiation in pricing and student selection. Quite naturally, the Ministry must operate within the limits of the political guidance it receives from government, and in the absence of wide political agreement only marginal policy adjustments available to a small number of institutions are possible. In addition, the Ministry has worked with employers and the HBO sector to introduce a new short-cycle qualification, which will add differentiation to mix of qualifications available to students.

While *hogescholen* instructors should ideally remain in close contact with working life, knowledgeable observers with whom we met expressed concern that this ideal is frequently not achieved, and that many HBO instructors – particularly those who have been teaching a long time - have too little contact with working life, and find it difficult to stay abreast of the changing knowledge base in their professional field.

The HBO system appears to offer far too little *flexible* provision – whether part-time, compressed delivery, dual learning, or other options. The Netherlands has adult education and training levels (16.9 participation rate among those 25-64) that are modestly above the EU-14 average, but well below those of the high-performing nations such as Finland, Denmark, and Sweden.

Hogescholen remain closely joined to a local employment mission, and have not fully responded to the opportunities presented by European and even global mobility of labour, the norm of European-wide professional employment, and the increased prospect of career changes throughout one's working life. None of our discussions with sectoral or institutional HBO elicited any mention of these developments in working life and their implications for the instructional mission of HBO institutions.

Notwithstanding the binary division of labour in the Netherlands, it is a fact of life that many institutions charged with providing *wetenschappelijk onderwijs* are in reality engaged in higher professional education - in the sense that their graduates will enter professional life, such as teaching or engineering, after the completion of their studies, rather than becoming scholars in universities, researchers in laboratories, or otherwise engaged in a life of scientific work. One unintended consequence of a binary division of labour may be that research universities and the wider society neglect the employability obligations and performance of research universities.

The Netherlands tertiary system has introduced *lectoren*, HBO-based research faculty who are responsible for leading knowledge circles (*kenniskringen*) within their institution and wider professional community. In the estimation of the HBO-Raad and the OCW this has been a successful initiative, evidence of which is furnished by an *effectmeting* (impact assessment) undertaken in 2006. The review team, however, takes a different view. We have two principal concerns about the *lectoren* initiative.

- First, the processes by which *lectoren* posts are allocated among and within HBO institutions broadly disperse these resources. This limits the capacity of this initiative to build a critical mass of sufficient depth and expertise for HBOs to function more effectively as innovation partners with firms and non-profit organizations.

- Second, we are concerned that the *lectoren* initiative has not been fully understood or exploited as a means by which to strengthen and vitalize the educational mission of HBO institutions. During our visit HBO institutions did not present us with a well-developed conception of how *lectoren* (and *kenniskringen*) might be used to as develop teaching and practice-led research - as opposed to research-led teaching. By this we have in mind a distinctive model of HBO research that takes place in an applied setting, that involves undergraduate students, and results not in international peer-reviewed publications, but instead in expert improvements to professional practice, whether new pupil assessments in primary or secondary schools, or newly-customized information systems for the international flower retail industry.

We think that the wider social interests of the Netherlands would be well served by *some* HBO institutions developing greater capacities as knowledge partners and centres of leadership and innovation in professional practice. We think this is not likely to be successfully accomplished through the *lectoren* initiative alone, but will require in addition wider collaboration across the binary line (outlined below, in point two), or through initiatives that lead to competitive "third stream funding" for applied and practice-oriented research (of the sort awarded through Finland's TEKES), through competitively awarded sabbaticals for HBO instructors to renew their professional ties and knowledge, and through a career system that evaluates and strongly rewards professional engagement.

6.4 Recommendations

In light of the challenges described above, we propose three initiatives be given consideration.

1. To address the weakness of the tertiary system with respect to flexible provision, we believe that much wider scope for alternative providers needs to be considered. We recognise that an *open bestel* initiative is underway. We think it likely that a sharp shift in flexible provision may require strong competition to traditional tertiary providers – including competition from for-profit providers of higher education that specialise in flexible provision. To this end, we think that a review committee, containing representatives from the OCW and NVAO, but also the Ministry of Economic Affairs and the CPB, should generate proposals for providing maximum market entry opportunities consistent with consumer protection, and explore the means by which to allow the full state subsidy (including institutional operating subsidy and student support) to be applied towards study at such a provider. The purpose of such an initiative is to create a dynamic in the system that is presently lacking.

2. Second, to strengthen professionally oriented bachelor education - in both the HBO and WO sectors that are in fact providing it - we recommend that collaborative arrangements and couplings of units from both sectors be strongly encouraged by the OCW. For example, while maintaining separate organisations – since these are necessary for distinctive HBO activities such as continuing education, short-cycle degrees, and flexibly accelerated study programmes, and research programmes and graduate instruction in the WO institution - joint programmes in study lines such as business, teaching, public administration and social services could be encouraged. These could be hosted by a separate organisation (*e.g.* college), and bring to bear the comparative expertise of HBO programmes (work-based learning, employability focus, and employer engagement) with the comparative advantage of WO institutions (research training and experience of WO instructors, wider national and international engagement of their institution) in the creation of a new study option. To spur innovations of this sort,

the NVAO should provide an experimental waiver of regulatory restricts, applying an *ex post* assessment based upon a careful analysis of student evaluations, employer interviews, and labour market outcomes. For its part, the OCW should provide funding incentives (*e.g.* apply the more generous of the funding methodologies used for HBO and WO), and one-off funding, awarded on a competitive basis, to support the costs of such an initiative. In the long run, we anticipate that such an initiative would need to be permitted some opportunity to distinctive position itself in the system - with respect to nomenclature, pricing, and selection, so as to make itself a sustainable quality initiative.

3. Finally, we recommend that a disinterested and expert third party undertake the assessment of the *lectoren* initiative planned for 2008. In our view, the Netherlands CPB may be best suited to this role.

7. *Research and Innovation*

7.1 Background

Three successive Dutch cabinets have expressed their commitment to the Lisbon strategy and their desire to promote the Dutch knowledge economy as one of the most successful in Europe by 2010. This commitment has led to the setting of technology and innovation policy agendas. In 2003 the white paper on human resources in science and engineering (*Deltaplan beta en techniek*) was prepared as a joint effort of three ministries (OECD, 2004b, p. 15). It promotes courses in science and technology at all levels of education and conducts a number of projects in tertiary education and innovation in order to promote the image of technology and stimulate regional action plans.

As noted in Chapter Three, in September 2003 the cross-Ministry Innovation Platform, chaired by the Prime Minister, was established in order to develop strategic plans for promoting the Dutch knowledge economy and enhancing innovation. The mission of the Innovation Platform is 'to strengthen the innovation potential of the Netherlands in order to secure a leading role for this country in the European knowledge economy of 2010', in part by re-establishing 'values such as excellence, ambition and entrepreneurship'. Like many other government initiatives in this field, the Innovation Platform is intended to stimulate co-operation between business enterprises and knowledge-creating institutions. Its 18 members are mostly selected from the business community and knowledge institutions. The model was taken from Finnish cabinet-level Science and Technology Policy Council. However there is an important difference in that the Dutch Innovation Platform doers not have a permanent legal status.

In recent years R&D investment in the Netherlands has not moved in a favourable direction. In 1999 R&D expenditure was 2.02% of GDP, below the OECD average; by 2002 it had declined to 1.72% compared to an OECD average of 2.25%. Whereas the share of higher education and government R&D together was above the OECD average, 0.75% in the Netherlands compared with 0.64% in the OECD in 2003, R&D investment by the private sector at 1.0% was well below the OECD average of 1.5% (OECD, 2004c; van Steen *et al.*, 2004 and 2006).

Further, even in the public sector investment in R&D has declined, from 0.87% of GDP in 1998 to 0.77% in 2002 (OCW, 2006b, p. 123).

As noted in Chapter Three, the Netherlands is strong in basic research and has an excellent record in scientific publication. Scientific articles per capita are 6th highest in the OECD (*OECD Science, Technology and Industry Scoreboard 2005*) and in 2002-2003 its average citation score was 26% above the world average in 2000-2003 (NOWT, 2005, p. 18; see also van Steen *et al.*, 2004, p. 84). The main share of research articles, 69%, is produced by scientists and scholars employed at the 13 research intensive universities (NOWT, *ibid.*, p. 17). The Netherlands ranks number three among a set of benchmark countries with an average output of almost one publication per researcher per year in the public sector (NOWT, *ibid,* p. 17). Private sector researchers in the Netherlands are also highly productive, owing in large part to the publication output of the corporate laboratories of the Dutch multinational enterprises, especially Philips whose central research laboratories are located in Eindhoven. The situation may change in the future because some of these central laboratories are being dismantled.

The Netherlands ranks well on EPO high-tech patent applications. It is second after Finland in a comparison of 21 countries (OECD, 2005b), though is about average in USPTO high-tech patents granted. Overall, the Netherlands has been assessed to have an excellent record in knowledge creation but a mediocre one in innovation, defined as successful development and application of new knowledge in new products and/or processes. As noted, this profile is referred to as the 'Dutch paradox'. The proportion of innovative enterprises that co-operate with higher education institutions and with research institutes is relatively low in the Netherlands as compared with other EU15 countries, though it has increased significantly in the 2000s (OCW, 2004a; van Steen *et al.*, 2006). A smaller share of innovative Dutch manufacturing companies considers universities as an important supplier of knowledge than is the case in Europe as whole (1% as compared with 4% average according to OECD, 2003, p. 9).

The low level of Business Enterprise Research and Development (BERD) can be explained in part with reference to the industrial structure of the country. First, the share of services within the economy is relatively high and the share of high intensive R&D manufacturing relatively low. Second, seven major multinational companies are responsible for roughly 50% of the BERD conducted in the Netherlands (van Steen *et al.*, 2004, p. 24). The R&D intensity of Dutch industry is heavily dependent on R&D expenditure in these companies; foreign direct investments in R&D in the Netherlands are relatively small. Despite the excellence of university research the Netherlands is not attracting foreign enterprises to invest in R&D on a sufficient scale. Some anecdotal evidence provided to the review team also suggested that an increasing proportion of Dutch-owned multinational R&D was taking place abroad. This would be consistent with the general trend to the internationalisation of R&D, but it is noted that the Ministry of Economic Affairs finds that 'there is no evidence … that large Dutch enterprises are relocating R&D to foreign countries' (Ministry for Economic Affairs, 2006, pp. 36-37).

In 2005 only seven Netherlands-based companies spent more than EUR 100 million on R&D. Philips is much the largest player at EUR 1 001 million, followed by Azko Nobel (EUR 425 million), ASML at 348 million and Shell at 239 million (*Top 30 Bedrijfs-R&D un Nederland 2005*, data supplied by VNO-NCW). Table 7.1 lists the top ten companies:

Table 7.1 Principal Netherlands-based company expenditure on R&D in 2005

Company and location	R&D spending 2005
	million EUR
Philips, Eindhoven	1 001
Azko Nobel, Arnhem	425
ASML, Veldhoven	348
Shell, Amsterdam/Rijswijk	239
DSM, Geleen/Delft	163
Unilver, Vlaardingen	140
Oce, Venlo	130
Thales, Hengelo	63
Corus, Umuiden	62
Stork, Naarden	61

Source: VNO-NCW

Though the share of small and medium enterprises (SMEs) in R&D has increased, only a small portion of SMEs conduct R&D. It is estimated that 2% of SMEs have their own R&D unit, 28% carry out development, and 40% apply new knowledge and can be innovative (source: Joke van der Bandt: VNO-NCW).

This suggests that there might be more scope for expanding university-private sector links among small knowledge-intensive companies than large companies. Here, though 'the Netherlands also has a relatively small share of high-tech and medium high-tech sectors in the total economy' (van Steen *et al.*, 2004, p. 95). The problem is partly one of relative incentives given the success of the economy on other fronts. As long as Dutch entrepreneurs generate revenues in successful service-sector businesses with low R&D intensity they are unlikely to switch into R&D applications involving large sunk costs, long lead times and uncertainty.

All national research systems are faced with the challenge of global competition between nations in relation to what has become a semi-globalised worldwide research system. The Netherlands faces particular difficulties in securing national objectives and even in imposing a national policy template. As noted university-industry co-operation in R&D depends upon a small number of few multinational firms that are only partly Netherlands-based. To the extent that these Dutch multinationals expand their partnerships with universities around the world there are fewer opportunities for Dutch universities.

The processes of economic, political and educational Europeanisation introduce a third, regional dimension with possibilities for university R&D. The European Research Area has catalysed new mechanisms of integration within the European research landscape. These include consortia among research partners and emerging mechanisms for joint research funding by national funding agencies. These trends create new possibilities for the development of research capabilities in higher education institutions while also exposing them to additional competition. Further, and significantly given the 'Dutch paradox', European projects also provide an important additional medium for university-industry collaboration. Here the industry partners may be located in countries outside the Netherlands and the knowledge economy benefits may flow outside the country but remain in Europe. At this point both university research, and the university-industry relationship, are not narrowly embedded in the Dutch national policy context, but operate within a much wider setting.

It is likely that in future years the European dimension will increasingly affect the conduct and utility of research conducted in Dutch higher education, will alter incentives and policy objectives and will prompt a reworking of programmes designed to bring universities and industry closer together. However, the review team was unable to access data on the extent to which Dutch research organizations and enterprises currently participate in European schemes so as to more closely investigate this emerging and transformative area. There was no indication that these challenges were being addressed at policy level.

The Netherlands Organisation for Scientific Research, NWO, is the most important funding agency for basic research. It maintains research institutes of its own and awards funding to research carried out at universities. It supports research programmes, individuals, investments in equipment and facilities, and travel and international cooperation (van Steen *et al.*, 2004, pp. 19-20). Together with the Royal Academy of Sciences (KNAW), it is the main source of Stream 2 funding to universities, which as noted in Chapter Three, is awarded competitively according to academic criteria. NWO has proved its ability to think and act strategically so as to improve higher education research in the Netherlands. It is an important national asset.

NWO recently released a strategy for its activities in 2007-2010, based on two policy stances: the promotion of excellence, and better utilization of knowledge to strengthen societal and technological innovation. The plan relies on doubling the funds of NWO as part of national fulfilment of the Lisbon goals. The NWO already promotes research excellence and utilization of knowledge. The allocation of project money by using peer review is an example of the former; while the Technology Foundation STW, part of the NWO, is an example of the latter. The Foundation supports university research in science and technology. It actively supports knowledge utilization through users' committees. For each project a users' committee is appointed, which closely monitors the progress of the project and advises the STW Board especially in relation to utilization of the findings. These committees include as members business enterprise representatives. The committees serve as a forum for communication, and potentially, as an instrument of utilization, if an enterprise is prepared to develop the results commercially. NWO will also collaborate with SenterNovem in the new SmartMix scheme (see below).

Schemes for university-industry co-operation have a dual purpose: to promote the utilisation of scientific research results in the development of new products or processes and to enhance the ability to generate new scientific research questions emerging from innovation activities. The Dutch government has launched a significant number of such schemes. Some date back to the early 80s. The schemes are based on different approaches:

- Programme-based schemes such as the Leading Technological Institutes, Innovation-Oriented Research Programmes and public-private programmes in specific fields such as genomics and catalysis;

- Applied research institutes such as TNO, the agricultural research institutes and the Large Technological Institutes are set up as knowledge transfer institutes to further the application of basic research in society. TNO is under the auspices of the Ministry of Education, Culture and Science and receives a basic grant from this ministry. TNO receives targeted grants from several other ministries. The targeted grant from the Ministry of Economic Affairs has the condition of co-funding by businesses. TNO has 24 knowledge centres in which it co-operates with universities and businesses and 50 university professors work in part-time positions at TNO. There are project-based schemes for R&D co-operation with special attention to SMEs. The group of large technological institutes consists of five specialised organisations conducting applied research and related activities in specific fields. The main funding scheme is contract funding by public and private parties.

– Support for knowledge infrastructures, includes a scheme to subsidise knowledge infrastructures in public-private consortia in areas of societal importance.

A useful discussion of Dutch schemes to promote public-private partnerships is provided in a report prepared by the OECD (OECD, 2003). As noted recent measures to promote public-private co-operation include SmartMix. This is a 100 million Euro scheme that commences in 2007 with the objective of promoting university-industry collaboration. SenterNovem, an intermediary organization under the Ministry of Economic Affairs and NWO, the research council funded by the Ministry of Education, Culture and Science, will manage it.

Some schemes to promote the utilisation of research results specifically address the improvement of knowledge utilisation in SMEs. These initiatives are noteworthy, reflecting a willingness to find solutions to problems that have been detected. With the so-called "knowledge voucher" SMEs can buy research services from universities and from other types of institute including large firms, 'in order to improve the innovation of processes, products and services' (Background Report, p. 27). The value of the large "knowledge voucher" is EUR 7 500, of which SMEs should contribute one third themselves. As of 2006, there will also be smaller knowledge vouchers representing a value of EUR 2 500 which stimulates SMEs to become acquainted with research institutes ('sniffing vouchers') (van Steen *et al.*, 2006, p. 68). At the commencement of the scheme the number of vouchers was 100. Following initial demand it was increased to 6 000. 'Many employers have been using this subsidy and relations with knowledge institutes have been intensified' (Background Report, p. 28).

Another example is the RAAK-regulation, the Regional Action and Attention for Knowledge Innovation. This involves EUR 6-8 million per year and is intended to strengthen the relationship between SMEs and higher education institutions, in particular the HBOs. The Regulation provides financial support to co-operative projects. Nearly half of the total project funds come from co-operating SMEs.

In addition the HBOs have been provided with *lectoren*. This programme began in 2001; in 2006 it was funded at the level of EUR 38.4 million and this will increase to EUR 50 million in 2007. The number of posts has grown rapidly, from 18 in 2002 to 207 in 2005 and now 270 (Background Report, p. 12), and the programme has attracted much attention. *Lectoren* are to respond to the knowledge needs of SMEs and to enhance research skills and capabilities in HBOs by conducting research projects to which faculty are recruited on a part-time basis. Though only 5% of the teaching staff in HBOs now holds doctorates, this proportion will probably increase due in part to the *lectoren* scheme. Individual lectors are expected to create 'knowledge circles' with the SMEs with which they co-operate in the projects. RAAK programme money is typically used in these projects.

The *lectoren* programme appears to be advancing its aims, though it may be some of concern that there is little cooperation between the *lectoren* and the research universities. In future it will extend the stimulation of research activities in the HBO sector. 'From 2007 onwards HBOs will receive funds for development and application, or applied research, as a follow-up of payment for the lectoren' (*Background Report*, p. 66).

7.2 Strengths

Overall scientific performance and knowledge production in the Netherlands is very good, sustained by a culture of excellence and excellent connectivity within worldwide research systems. International review committees have conducted periodic reviews of research excellence since the 1970s and these reviews have helped to shape priorities. Bad reviews have led to retrenchment of activities. This has conveyed a strong signal about the importance of excellence that has no doubt influenced the behaviour of individual researchers and institutions. The review team perceives the value of this kind of quality control and recommends its continuation. Likewise national reviews since the early 1990s, conducted so as to determine allocations of the label 'excellent research schools', have sustained the drive to genuine excellence even though no financial consequences are involved (Sonneveld and Oost, 2006). Researchers are at least as strongly motivated by peer respect and esteem as by revenues.

Overall, the Dutch research system is relatively internationalised. In general Dutch research groups emphasise internationalisation and the building of international reputation, cross-border collaboration, and publication in international journals, and many have very successful track records (Sonneveld and Oost, 2006, pp. 12-13). As is discussed further in Chapter Nine, the Dutch university system employs university staff from other countries in reasonable numbers and many universities have enrolled significant numbers of foreign research students and offered positions to foreign post-doctoral scholars. This indicates the attractiveness of the Dutch system, despite immigration barriers. In addition Dutch students and graduates are encouraged to spend time abroad especially at the postdoctoral stage.

The review team formed the view that national policies, programmes and coordination in the area of research and innovation might be stronger than national policies in most other areas. Policies on research and innovation appear to be less subject to short term politicisation, are more likely to involve effective consultation, and are more likely to make use of advanced expertise and data gathering in the processes of planning and policy design.

7.3 Weaknesses

Although the overall graduation rate in research degrees in the Netherlands, 1.4‰ population in 2004, is competitive in relation to the OECD average of 1.3 (OECD, 2006a, p. 58), the position in science and technology is less good. Among 25-34 year olds the number of doctorates in these fields in the Netherlands is 0.4‰ population compared to 1.5 in Sweden and 0.9 in the USA and the UK (OCW, 2006d, p. 7). The low total numbers of researchers per thousand workforce suggests a relatively low overall R&D in the Netherlands. In 2004 there were 5.2 in the Netherlands as compared with 6.6 in Germany and France, 10.1 for Sweden and 13.7 for Finland.

In addition, 'the Netherlands has not been very successful in attracting and retaining foreign human resources in science and technology (HRST). Not only are HRST immigration flows relatively low, but such immigrants also tend not to stay in the Netherlands, regarding it as a stepping-stone to other destinations' (OECD, 2006b, p. 117). (Problems of attracting and holding foreign faculty and researchers in the context of immigration issues and other problems are discussed further in Chapter Nine).

These problems are likely to worsen unless corrective action is taken. The review team noted problems in the career system in universities. Most researchers seem to follow a path-dependent course, and there is little scope for incentive payments. The nation lacks a robust internal market for talent and is unable to function as a strong attractor of external talent. Yet careers in science do not attract enough outstanding young people. Anecdotal evidence suggests that salaries and job security are likely to be contributing factors; and that over a long period the relative lack of opportunities for tenured employment has accumulated a significant disincentive effect, so that not enough students studying science at school imagine for themselves a career in research. Long lag times before younger faculty have the opportunity to develop their own research programmes without being supervised by a senior professor are another factor. In the USA promising researchers are able to shape their own pathways at an earlier stage. The NWO programmes, particularly the Veni and Vidi awards, have attempted to address this and are a step in the right direction, as universities are obliged to give some kind of guaranteed position to awardees. However, these targeted initiatives do not sufficiently address the underlying career problems facing most young researchers in the Dutch university career system.

7.4 Recommendations

The Committee on the dynamics of university research concluded that 'the interaction between the university research system and non-university research centres is neither better nor worse than in other – comparable – countries', though it also remarked that 'existing distrust between government, universities and companies' should be eliminated. It suggested that 'universities should abandon their defensive positions and clearly formulate their contribution to the future of the Netherlands' (van Steen *et al., 2006,* p. 28). The OECD team endorses these remarks, which would be relevant to most national innovation systems.

Although Dutch universities exhibit a strong orientation to excellence this might need to become more strategically focused. There is a need to better understand the institutional conditions under which 'peaks' of excellence thrive, as opposed to 'mounds'. As suggested in Chapter Three it is likely that universities carrying front rank research capacity across many disciplines provide the best environment for high performance, especially but not only in cross-disciplinary activities. In addition such universities can maximise both the status power and the resource power sufficient to attract and hold the highest calibre scholar-researchers and doctoral students. This points to the potential offered by national policies designed to elevate a small number of universities to a stronger position within the Shanghai Jiao Tong ranking.

As noted in Chapter Three, increasing the share of research support that is allocated on the basis of competitive bids for programmes, people and projects and determined on the ground of excellence can install a stronger competitive driver in the funding system. Whether it is determined by past research performance or not, block funding cannot have the same effect. It is proposed that the proportion of evaluation-based and competitive resource allocation (Stream 2) within the research funding system be increased so as to foster excellence and concentration - provided that this increase is accompanied by a change to Stream 2 allocations so as to ensure that these cover a higher proportion of research costs. At present universities must match every one euro in research subsidy they receive in Streams 2 and 3 with 84 cents of matching funding from the basic grant (AWT, 2005, p. 13). If they are 'too successful' at raising funding determined by competition and excellence they find themselves matching at more than one to one euro level. This creates a disincentive to engage in such research, and also reduces the scope for university determined research initiatives including projects in the humanities and social sciences. These problems are now widely recognised within government and the research organisations (*Background Report*, p. 66).

Nonetheless such an increase in the role of Stream 2 funding should be managed cautiously. It is emphasised that if policy is to increase the emphasis on funding based on competition and excellence (in a research funding system that is already competitive) it is of the utmost importance that the internal balance between foundation funding and variable funding is monitored, in order to ensure that the global strength of Dutch universities in basic research is sustained and enhanced. In the term used by AWT, university research is most usefully considered as an 'asset', as a form of knowledge capacity with open-ended long term potential, with utilities that cannot always be predicted in advance, rather than as a set of 'products' (AWT, 2005). Maintaining this asset requires a solid foundation derived from the basic funding in Stream 1. Policy approaches that would reduce the asset base supported by Stream 1, attempt to prescribe research activity in detail, and/or depart from peer definition of excellence, would be destructive.

Ideally Stream 2 funding would cover the full additional costs of the research with a concurrent reduction in that proportion of Stream 1 funding that is variable. It would be better if policy moved in that direction. This is more important given that it is unclear that institutions actually allocate all of the Stream 1 monies to research, as these monies are incorporated into their block grants from government (in that respect the Streams 1-3 formula probably overestimates the extent of public support for research). If financial pressures increase, a growing part of Stream 1 funding will be siphoned off for other purposes.

Another reason for expanding Stream 2 funding rather than Stream 1 funding is that at present the social partners are not confident that extra money put into the system via Stream 1 would be well used for research purposes. For example, there is no guarantee that it would be used to promote research concentration and excellence, the more so given that many universities do not seem to have the strategic capabilities to plan and implement change.

Such a change in national research funding should be followed by the application of similar principles in the internal resource allocation of universities themselves. According to evidence presented to the review team, at present internal allocations typically follow previous allocations. A shift towards Stream 2 would enable greater concentration ('focus and mass'), more precise and extensive rewards for excellence; and the shaping of a national division of labour between research universities.

It is vital to attract talented students to science and technology fields and to careers in science and technology in order to help renew the research labour force, as well as for developing innovation and excellence. Attracting foreign direct investments in research and development is related to a county's ability to supply trained scientists and engineers for research jobs. The Innovation Research Incentives Scheme developed under the aegis of NWO provides three programmes of grants titled respectively Veni for postdoctoral awards, Vidi for early mid career personnel, and Vici for senior researchers. The primary focus of the scheme, as well as developing excellent projects, is to attract younger researchers ones to research careers (Veni), to hold them before they have obtained tenure (Vidi) and to provide additional opportunities for them through the teams established by senior researchers (Vici). (van Steen *et al.*, 2004, p. 52). The scheme has been well designed and could be usefully expanded.

There are a variety of mechanisms through which university research can be valorised. These include the traditional function of training personnel, public-private partnerships, spin-off formation, and patents & licensing. The review team did not obtain information of the effectiveness of the intellectual property rights regulations or any systematic information of the formation of spin-off firms from university research. However it was noted that some institutions house on-campus spin-off firms co-operating with the institution. Whether these provisions are effective for promoting spin-off formation is not known. However, the review team emphasises the importance of adequate conditions for the utilisation and the commercialization of research results via the formation and growth of spin-off firms.

As noted there are a number of programmes and mechanisms designed to address utilisation through public-private partnerships. Some date back over twenty years, though most are fairly recent. The evaluation of the effectiveness of each of these measures is outside the remit of the review team. These initiatives together represent a positive trend. Nevertheless the review team noted that there is almost an overabundance of interventions and initiatives to promote university-private partnerships. It appears that the outcome has been a system that is not easy or transparent for stakeholders. The review recommends that the system be simplified and made more easily usable for potential research partners.

One way to unify and systematise the policy contribution of the different instruments in the system, is to introduce a common set of principles that cut across the different programmes that further public-private partnerships. For example, in Finland large companies can get Tekes[14] funding for their R&D projects provided that those projects fulfil at least one of the five standard criteria. One criterion is cooperation with SMEs or research organisations (universities or public research institutes), and another criterion is international cooperation. This means that government does not have to introduce a separate new programme every time it wants to advance specific aims; instead it can tweak the general principles operating across all programmes. It is possible that the 'Innovation omnibus' being developed by the Ministry of Economic Affairs in relation to its programmes in innovation will help to provide such a framework (van Steen *et al.*, 2006, p. 67). It is hoped that the 'omnibus' will assist the clarification, transparency, coordination and targeting of what has become a complex system of support for innovation.

It has been expected that the knowledge needs of SMEs should be largely met by the HBOs. Though there are good grounds to assume that local partnerships between HBOs and SMEs have great potential, the notion that SME needs will be sufficiently served by HBOs is based on a limited notion of SME needs. The question suggested here is, have the knowledge needs of high-tech SMEs been adequately addressed? The formation of university spinoffs in areas of emerging new technologies is a valuable route to valorisation of university research, and provides an example of SMEs with highly sophisticated knowledge needs. The review team received very little information on how the system works in this respect.

The programme to develop the research capabilities of HBOs through the *lectoren* system is a sensible initiative - provided that these resources are directed towards developing a research role that *enriches professional education* rather than a pale imitation of basic research in the WOs. However it is important to note that the resources required to properly develop the research capacities of HBOs are very substantial given that these efforts almost start from scratch. In this context the *lectoren* system is scarcely more than a drop in the ocean and may simply constitute the equal distribution of scarcity.

---

[14]   Finnish Funding Agency for Technology and Innovation.

This suggests that it would be advisable to target resources and expand the system very selectively through a bid-based system oriented to the development of research in the HBOs. The aim would be to create competitive research environments and promote strategic thinking in HBOs. The aim should be an incremental building up of research capacities. In this process, HBOs should obtain resources and abilities to attract young research-trained people to start their research programmes. These programmes should have a regional orientation and should be able to attract external money. This report will not recommend who should make the decisions on the competitive bids, but it is noted that a stakeholder organization has structural problems in attempting to perform such a function.

As noted the Innovation Platform was established in 2003 as a coordinating body to propose strategic plans in the promotion of the Dutch knowledge economy. This Platform has been informal and dependent on the personal commitment of the Prime Minister. Both Dutch Higher Education and the Dutch research and innovation system are faced with many difficult decisions and ambitious objectives related to focus and mass in research, research excellence, utilisation of research results, the development of human resources and the enhancement of public awareness. There is a continuing need for a coordinating platform with sufficient status and impetus to make a difference. Thus suggests that the Innovation Platform should be formalized and made permanent.

This in turn would provide a continuing forum in which important stakeholders could discuss, and reach consensus on the different future options. Some of the reforms proposed here are not feasible in the absence of joint commitment by the stakeholders. There is a need to increase trust different social stakeholders feel towards each other, and a joint forum is an excellent means towards this end. The review recommends that the original model for the Platform, that of the Science and Technology Policy Council of Finland, be considered more fully. In addition, there is a continuing need to further co-operation and coordination within government. This suggests that it would be valuable to add the Minister of Finance to the other ministers in the Platform, and perhaps other ministers with an interest in research activities.

8. *Quality Assurance and Quality Enhancement*

8.1 Background

For fifteen years until 2002, the quality assurance process for higher education in the Netherlands was a system of peer review. This included a self-assessment document prepared by the institution, followed by a site visit by a group of peers organised either by the Association of Universities or the Association of Hogescholen, depending on type of institution. The results of this process on each discipline were made public and the Minister had the right to step in if there were identified problems that might require external intervention. It was argued that this process was focused less on accountability and more on the improvement of programmes.

However, whilst the reports were published, many felt that the evaluation was not sufficiently independent or objective. Moreover possible interventions were limited to publicly funded institutions.

As the Netherlands introduced the Bachelor and Masters degrees, there was a change in the quality assurance process, with a movement towards external accreditation of programmes to reflect the wider international context. The stated aim for accreditation was to provide assurance to all stakeholders in the quality and standards of the awards offered in all higher education institutions delivering Netherlands awards. In part national accreditation was a implemented in response to the 1999 Bologna declaration which identified certain expectations of higher education in Europe, including quality assurances processes.

The Accreditation Organisation of The Netherlands and Flanders (NVAO) was established by law as the accrediting body, with responsibility for the accreditation of all bachelors and masters programmes from publicly funded institutions, and private institutions wishing to offer degree programmes. NVAO is a body independent of Government, although its activities are legally reviewable.

NVAO's role is both to conduct the accreditation process; and to recognise and oversee the role of the private commercial organisations

(VBIs) which act as assessors of institutional applications prior to submission to NVAO. VBIs develop their own frames of reference for conducting the assessment of each application for accreditation, evaluating institutions against the accreditation criteria. One such mechanism developed by a VBI focuses in the first instance on the institution as a whole before looking at the programme to be accredited. Each institution chooses one or more VBIs to suit its own requirements although for historical reasons HBOs are more likely to ask the National Qualifications Agency (NQA) which originated with the HBO-Raad, and universities the Quality Assurance Netherlands Universities (QANU) which developed from the university branch organisation. There are also organisations that have been set up as VBIs, some of which are consultancies with experience in other aspect of higher education such as accountancy and management. VBIs are assessed by NVAO every two years or so to ensure that they are operating appropriately. NVAO also has annual meetings of all the VBIs to discuss matters of mutual interest such as the report writing structure.

Each programme is accredited every six years. The criteria used to evaluate a submission for accreditation are aims and objectives, programme, deployment of staff, facilities and provisions.

The accreditation process for existing programmes starts with an internal management review followed by the production of a self-assessment by the institution. This self-assessment is submitted to the VBI along with supporting documentation. The institution can ask for special quality features to be considered which may result in the report stating that the course indeed has special features. A team of assessors visits the institution from the VBI who will meet with staff and students to evaluate the submission.

Once the process has been completed the VBI makes a recommendation to NVAO explaining how their view is based on the facts, the VBI's analysis of the facts and the assessment of the degree course on the basis of the given accreditation framework and the VBI's own frame of reference (from NVAO guide, 2006)

Once a submission has been received by NVAO, it is committed to publishing its decision within three months. For new programmes the Ministry takes a decision on the macro efficiency as a next step: The publicly funded submissions are sent to the Ministry for a 'macro-efficiency' review to establish whether or not the programme will provide graduates that will benefit the country, as noted in Chapter Three. The final decision is made within three months. An unsuccessful application for accreditation means that an institution cannot offer a new programme, or has to cease offering an existing programme, although NVAO has the capacity to suggest that an institution takes a little longer to develop a submission if it is clear that it will not be successful. It has been proposed that the 'macro-efficiency' decision for new programmes will be made prior to the accreditation decision so that the expense of accreditation is not incurred if the Ministry rejects the programme; however, legislation containing this proposal was withdrawn from parliamentary consideration.

As part of the Ministry there is an inspectorate that has responsibility for all levels of education within the Netherlands. It is mainly concerned with the oversight of legal matters. The number of officers with responsibility for higher education has reduced since accreditation was introduced, suggesting a reduced role for the Inspectorate with respect of higher education. However, the Inspectorate does monitor some themes in higher education each year, for example assessment, and also has the responsibility for stepping in to review programmes or institutions if problems are identified. The inspectorate produces an annual report that provides a summary of education matters across the whole sector, in addition to publishing individual reports on themes, programmes and institutions as appropriate. The way in which problems with a particular programme or institution is identified was described to the team by the Inspectorate as being as a result of student complaints, staff complaints and/or press reports. In one particular example the impetus for the special report was a combination of complaints and press coverage.

Students have an opportunity to be involved in an annual overview of all programmes in tertiary education aimed at future students. For this purpose students are asked to complete a questionnaire to assess the quality of their programmes in a standard format.

This information, together with information from external peer reviews developed in the process of accreditation, is made available in both Dutch and English, at the website *studiekeuze123*.

Quality assurance for research was not changed in 2002. It is organised through the 'standards evaluation protocol for public research organisations' that is arranged by the branch organisations of the universities themselves. The protocol obliges all universities to evaluate their research activities every three years. Additionally, an independent external committee assesses the research activities and the outcomes of the external reviews are made public.

The criteria for accreditation require higher education institutions to have an internal quality assurance process that ensures: that degree courses are subject to periodic review partly based on verifiable targets, that have measure that can be demonstrated to improve the course and that will contribute to reaching the targets and that involve staff, students, alumni and the professional field in which graduates of the course are to be employed are actively involved in the internal quality assurance.

In the course of its visits to institutions, in discussions about internal quality assurance processes, the review team heard about how students are involved in the internal approval of new programmes and sit on internal central committees assisting in the development and oversight of the institution. It also heard that employers from appropriate fields are involved in course development in advisory capacities. The team was told that many HBOs have adopted the EFQM model of internal quality assurance that is an important development and has assisted the HBOs to achieve a clearer view of the way in which they conduct their business. The universities have not adopted the same model in the same way, but have, over a long period of time, developed mechanisms to deal with documentation and data to assist in their decision-making.

It is clear that successful accreditation can provide assurance that institutions meet the criteria that cover all aspects of quality assurance processes, and assure the coherence of the programme itself. In respect of the standards of awards the criterion on 'results' requires institutions to show that:

- Level has been achieved

  - The final qualifications that have been achieved correspond to the targets set for the final qualifications in level, orientation and domain specific requirements.

- Results of teaching

  - To measure the results of teaching target figures have been set in comparison with relevant other courses.

  - The results of teaching meet these targets.

The institution is therefore expected to have in place methods to ensure that students achieve the expected outcomes of the course.

However, the review team was told that there is no recognised and robust method of ensuring the security and independence of the marking or awarding process. The tutor who set the assessment can undertake the marking of student work. There is no expectation that the work might be subject to second or blind marking as a requirement of the process. The final decision on student awards is made by an examinations committee which, whilst it has to be independent from the management of the faculty, is made up of internal members of staff. The team heard of a perception that these committees come under pressure to make decisions to meet the demands of the institution, rather than making an objective decision based on available evidence. Whilst there is no evidence that anything other than objective and independent decisions are being made, the perception that there may be unhelpful influences on the final decision-making means that there is a problem in assuring all stakeholders that the final awards given are fair and reasonable.

8.2 Strengths

There are considerable strengths in the national quality assurance processes. The system of quality assurance has evolved to meet needs and in the process is learning from experience. It appears that when new needs appear the system has the personnel capacity, flexibility and good will to respond effectively. NVAO and the institutions have now accumulated significant expertise.

The criteria that are considered at each accreditation event would appear to focus on the right areas to provide assurance to all stakeholders that quality and standards are in place. In 2005, it was reported by the Inspectorate – in its overview report - that of the 55 accreditation submissions they checked, of some facets that were assessed as 'insufficient' in both HBO and universities, the key reasons were: assessment and control (18%), measures to improve quality (15%), output/efficiency of education (13%), volume of staff (9%), and, relationship between goals and the programme (9%).

8.3 Weaknesses

The review team heard from institutions that the process was very expensive both in terms of the amount of resource that was required to develop the self-assessment document, and the charges imposed by the VBI. The amounts quoted ranged from EUR 50 000 for one programme in a private institution, to EUR 500 000 for all programmes in one faculty to be accredited. The amount of resource to be put into the development of the accreditation will inevitably vary depending on the programme and the institution.

The 'macro-efficiency' test by the Ministry is a decision designed to prevent proliferation of similar/comparable programmes in places very near to each other. As the country moves towards 50% participation rate in higher education, it may wish to consider whether less micro control of the programmes on offer might encourage institutions to develop more innovative discipline areas that would appeal to students and new industries alike. Meaningful diversity in a discipline enhances the real options on offer. Universities should be free to take the risks of offering such programmes. In an enrolment based funding system it is they who bear the cost of such initiatives if students do not respond in sufficient numbers. In addition, in a knowledge economy in which participation is universally beneficial there is a case for saying that the subject matter of the degree might be of lesser importance than encouraging students to higher-level study.

8.4 Recommendations

The review team heard from higher education institutions that the accreditation process as originally devised and interpreted up to early 2006 is considered overly bureaucratic with too much emphasis on paperwork rather than a focus on enhancing the institution or the programme. Action has already been taken to try and reduce the demands of the process and to diminish the bureaucracy. However, the team also heard that in at least one institution there have been identified benefits flowing from the development of the self-assessment document and the institution considered that the process has helped them to evaluate their own provision. Whilst these developmental aspects are very important, and a key outcome from the self-assessment process, it is likely that the benefits will only be accrued the first time the process is undertaken. In a different institution the team heard that having had the provision of one school accredited, the financial commitment was such that no new programmes would be developed in the current period of accreditation.

It appears that the benefits to institutions flowing from the accreditation process will reduce over time and the associated bureaucracy will outweigh the potential developmental benefits. There is also the risk that new programme developments will be limited. Experience in other countries shows that institutions will quickly learn how to achieve successful accreditations without necessarily addressing all the necessary detail, turning what should be a developmental process into a formulaic engagement.

There has been discussion between the NVAO, the Government and the tertiary sector about what is to happen at the end of the six-year accreditation cycle. The view among higher education institutions is that that there should be a move to institutional accreditation. There is much merit in this proposal. It would build on a period of formal programme level accreditation, which is demonstrating to stakeholders that the health of programmes is good. Employer organisations are concerned that if programme level accreditation stopped there would no longer be any assurance that the programmes were still meeting the needs of the sector.

Most importantly, members of parliament show little enthusiasm for moving to institutional accreditation, and a recent proposal to do so has been withdrawn from parliamentary consideration.

If the Netherlands were to reconsider an institutional accreditation model, the NVAO would want to consider adopting methods different to the Inspectorate for identifying particular problems with programmes. Whilst problems identified in this way may provide the basis for undertaking special reviews, there is a risk that individuals will be encouraged to pursue particular grievances that may not be soundly based. The review team would recommend that as the processes for institutional accreditation and the inspectorate develop, there would be benefit in identifying more transparent and open criteria for generating specific reviews.

Given that the accreditation process is expensive for institutions one of the discussion points throughout the visit of the review team was how to best use the resources available to the sector. There are two areas where there might be benefit in reconsidering the process to address the matter of resources.

First, as it is likely that most of the beneficial aspects of accreditation have already been achieved, both in terms of institutional activity and success at accreditation; it may be possible to think of moving to institutional accreditation.

Second, a further cost-saving element might be reconsideration of the role of the VBIs. As commercial organisations the VBIs are, quite reasonably, looking to make a profit from the process. It is compulsory for all institutions to pay VBIs for their work towards accreditation and this money inevitably comes from public funding. It appears to be an anomaly that the recipients of profit from accreditation are commercial companies. It may be worth considering whether NVAO could appoint its own assessors and develop a method of assessing institutions not requiring the involvement of commercial companies. This would have the added benefit that if NVAO appointed assessors directly, the focus of the process could be more clearly based on peer review which is more familiar to those in higher education institutions. Further, such a procedure would streamline the whole process. It would mean that decisions would need to be made only once rather than, at present, twice, once by the VBI and once by NVAO.

In addition, it may be useful to consider the wider involvement of external, independent input into a number of internal processes. For example, examination committees could, with benefit, have an additional member who is an expert in the field but from another institution, and who could provide an independent view of the process and the award decisions made. This would assist in ensuring that the level achieved by students across the country is of a similar standard, and would have the benefit of providing assurance to staff and students that internal pressures have not unduly influenced the committees. Some countries have adopted a system of external examiners (for example the UK).

A further enhancement to the internal quality assurance procedures of higher education institutions could be the involvement of stakeholders in other internal development and review processes. Whilst the team heard that in institutions where the provision is largely vocational, employers are involved in the development of new awards, there was little evidence to show that external independent input was sought more generally. As institutions take more responsibility for their own awards, it may be useful to put in place an encouragement towards the greater involvement of external stakeholders in developing and reviewing awards in all discipline areas. The advantage of such involvement would be to provide an objective view of what is in place and would spread good practice. Such individuals could be specialists from other higher education institutions, from industry, the public services or international experts, all of whom would provide a new perspective on the way in which standards are set and maintained. The processes that would benefit from such an external view could range from initial development to course monitoring and periodic review, as well as the review of other activities such as learning resources.

9. The International Dimension

9.1 Background

Departmental statements and the websites of individual institutions emphasise commitments to comparative worldwide standing, the international orientation of curricula and the cross-border mobility of students. In practice the engagement with internationalisation is not as universal as this suggests.

First, as in all national systems, some Dutch tertiary institutions exhibit a largely or solely local orientation and are not particularly national in focus, let alone global. In itself this is no problem, being typical of all national education systems. Second, and more problematically, in the national system there is a more broadly based ambivalence towards the global dimension.

Tertiary education shares the two-sided relationship with the rest of the world that is distinctive of Dutch economy and society. This relationship was shaped in the building of an internationally competent trading nation prior to the present global era. In the 16th and 17th centuries Dutch internationalisation was profound for its time. At that time, cross-border relationships were mostly conducted at points of exchange in the national border zone, and the central institutions of national life were readily quarantined from global influences. In the present period, characterised by electronic global networking and frequent travel, global connections are not held at the border but run through the national heartland. This requires an internationalisation of a different kind in which varied cultures are in proximity within common systems.

The legacy of the old relationship with the outside world is contradictory. On one hand, higher education in the Netherlands can exhibit a high level of international awareness, openness, engagement and effectiveness in operating across borders - an effectiveness that many other nations might envy. At best, as in some of the academic departments of the research-intensive universities, personnel in the institutions have set aside all traces of a parochial or insular outlook and other factors that can inhibit global effectiveness at this time in any nation. Without losing confidence in their own distinctive Dutch strengths and a sense of core national project, they are not just economically open to the rest of the world but fully socially and culturally open as well. In that respect they can compete on equal terms anywhere in the world and have moved ahead of national policy makers to maximize the impact of Dutch education and research on the global stage. On the other hand, in both institutions and government there can be real limits to international curiosity and awareness in which the global dimension is simply blocked out.

Some personnel exhibit a 'business as usual' mentality amid the fast changing world environment. When people are in this frame of mind, the growing significance of global competition for knowledge intensive personnel is not grasped, and opportunities to develop Dutch institutions into more internationally relevant institutions (especially in the HBO sector) are missed. This is one reason why the need to hold local faculty stars or attract them back from abroad is not always recognised, and not enough thought is given to how to make Dutch tertiary education more attractive to foreign faculty and students. Despite the long association with the islands of Indonesia, and the excellence of Dutch university research in relation to that large, complex and geo-strategically significant nation, Dutch educational ties with Indonesia are surprisingly sparse. It is interesting to reflect on the Dutch lack of engagement with Indonesian education to the relatively close educational ties between on one hand the UK, on the other hand the South Asian countries, Malaysia and Singapore. However, recent policy documents, such as *Koers op Kwaliteit*, signal a rising interest in Southeast Asia, and seven of the county's ten priority countries identified in the document are located in South or East Asia (China, India, Malaysia, Thailand, Taiwan, and Vietnam). Additionally, Netherlands Educational Support Offices have been opened in Indonesia, China, Taiwan, and Vietnam (with a July 1, 2007 opening planned for a Thailand office).

The global standing of Dutch universities is not a product of marketing. The institutions are modest in promoting themselves internationally as institutions, although some individual academic units and research groups are effective. Rather this global standing has been earned solely by substantial achievements. Dutch research quality is often outstanding and in reputation Dutch universities are only short of the peak of universities worldwide in the USA and UK. Here the longstanding Dutch commitment to excellence in research and scholarship has paid global dividends. Further, Bologna compliance is ahead of most of Europe, as are English language skills. All of these factors create strategic advantages on the global scale.

This speaks well of the now established Dutch tradition of university self-management. Though there is inevitable unevenness there is much to be proud of and substantial resources with which to extend international engagement. Certainly Dutch universities and to a lesser extent the HBOs are already attractive to foreign students, particularly at the Masters and doctoral levels, and could attract many more.

Although Dutch students make good use of the ERASMUS schemes supporting shorter term mobility, when both numbers and duration of programme are taken into account, about three times as many foreign students come to the Netherlands to study as Dutch students going abroad. Within Europe the Netherlands is the sixth most important destination for Erasmus students, well behind Spain, France, the UK, Germany and Italy. Likewise the Netherlands has a presence in the global market in foreign students, but a lesser one in quantity terms, being the eighth largest European provider (data supplied by Ministry of Education Culture and Science). In 2002-2003 an estimated 37 000 foreign students were enrolled in public and accredited private institutions. Nearly half were from other European nations, including 22% from Germany, 10% Belgium, 5% Spain and 3% the UK. Another 10% were from Morocco, 5% from each of Turkey and Surinam, 4% China and 3% Indonesia. The 2004 proportion of all students in degree granting institutions who were foreign students was 4.0%, which was significantly below the OECD average of 8.0% and the EU19 average of 6.8%. The growth of foreign student numbers in Netherlands tertiary education since 2000 was 52%, the same as for the OECD as a whole (OECD, 2006a, p. 303).

Foreign students tend to play the largest role in Dutch universities at the postgraduate stage. For example at Technical University Delft in 2005, 53% of all doctoral students (663 persons) and 27% of all Masters students (835) were foreign students compared to 6% (648) at Bachelor level (data supplied by Marga Vintges, TU Delft Faculty of Engineering, 1 May, 2006). The majority of Dutch Masters programmes are offered in English. About 20% of all doctoral students are foreign students (Background Report, p. 86) and they can prepare their dissertations in either Dutch or English. Foreign doctoral student entry is very significant in some disciplines; for example approximately 50% of doctoral students in physics, and in fields such as electronics in some universities the ratio is higher.

Whereas the Netherlands is successful in holding as knowledge workers many students originating from Eastern European nations after they have graduated in the Netherlands, it appears to be less successful than the USA, UK and Australia in holding graduates who originated from India and China.

If the economic cost alone is taken into account, Dutch universities ought to be able to attract a substantial flow of students from the UK into

English-language postgraduate programmes. Tuition charges for EU students under 30 years of age are EUR 1 445 compared to a minimum of EUR 4 250 in the UK. In addition many EU students are eligible for a rebate of EUR 1 000 and so pay only EUR 500 for tuition in the Netherlands. Non-EU foreign student tuition charges are much higher in the Netherlands but are still competitive vis-à-vis the USA and UK. A two-year Masters of Science in Chemical Engineering at Delft University of Technology, which costs EU citizens EUR 1 445, costs a non-EU citizen EUR 8 150 (data from the Observatory on Borderless Education, 2006).

On the other hand there is a relatively small number of doctoral scholarships for foreign students, in part because the predominant model of doctoral education is employment rather than scholarship based. Perhaps university personnel are more reluctant to provide such employment for foreigners. But competition for outstanding doctoral students is a key aspect of the global knowledge economy. Here the Netherlands is uncompetitive compared to the United States, where two thirds of doctoral students receive scholarship support (data from the Institute for International Education, 2006). Approximately one quarter of foreign students in the Netherlands are offered scholarships through an international granting agency, a Dutch programme or their home countries. However 83% of these scholarships go to Europeans, with 12% to Asia and just 3% to Africa (data from the Observatory on Borderless Education, 2006).

According to the OECD 25.1% of Dutch citizens students who go abroad to study enrol in Belgium, 20.1% enrol in the UK, 15.3% in Germany, 12.3 in the USA, 5.2% to Sweden and 5.0% to France (OECD, 2006a, pp. 308-309). Approximately 6% of all Dutch students in both kinds of university participate in cross-border mobility each year. A significant minority of graduates, 26% from HBOs and 39% from research universities, have had some kind of foreign experience (Background Report, p. 86) though much of this consists of short programmes.

According to the departmental Background Report (p. 86) an estimated 25% of all faculty members in the research universities have foreign origins but the proportion in the HBOs is just 3%. As in other nations (Enders and de Weert, 2004) the main internationalisation of faculty is comprised by short-term leave, exchange visits and research collaboration. A total of 38% of all knowledge workers in the research universities had foreign experience in the previous five years with three fifths spending time in Europe and two fifths in the USA.

This pattern of faculty visits matches the patterns of co-authorship of scientific papers. About three papers in five are co-authored in Europe, including 11.3% in each of the UK and Germany, 6.6% in France and 5.5% in each of Italy and Belgium (OCW, 2004a, p. 87).

Where longer term faculty mobility is strong, it takes the form of the exit of talented researchers and scholars at the doctoral and post-doctoral stage, especially to the USA; it signals a loss of national capacity that will have accumulating effects. The Netherlands shares the problem of net brain drain with many other advanced nations but unlike some other nations is not doing much about it. The issue is widely acknowledged but little addressed.

The government provides Netherlands Education Support Offices in some countries. A number of universities have established joint foreign university institutes where persons from the universities concerned can study the country of location, persons from abroad can study Dutch language and culture, and scholars from the two nations can meet and exchange knowledge and perspectives. The universities of Leiden, Utrecht, Nijmegen, Groningen and Leuven jointly govern such an institute in Cairo. Other institutes jointly governed by Leiden and other universities are situated in Rome, Istanbul and Tokyo. Other institute is located in St Petersburg, Florence, Madrid, Athens, Morocco, Turkey, and Syria. Some larger HBOs are establishing foreign campuses. There was little discussion of this in OCW or the HBO sector. The British and Australian experience of offshore operations suggests that it is important to establish effective quality audit and assurance in relation to such programmes. Offshore operations are by their nature less transparent than programmes on home soil and are not routinely compared to other programmes. In this case the dynamic of natural self-regulation, on which much real quality maintenance depends, needs more supplementation by formal regulatory process than is the case with local Dutch programmes.

Leiden is one of the most internationalised universities in the world. It often leads collaborative meetings, consortia and other initiatives involving cross-border networks. For example the Leiden University International Institute of Asian Studies, which is frequently visited by outstanding foreign scholars, houses a concentration of expertise that has few equals anywhere. In comparison with comparable centres in the English-speaking institutions the Institute is particularly notable for the breadth and depth of expertise in language and dialect. Asian Studies at Leiden is only one field in which particular concentrations of Dutch scholar researchers have an outstanding international presence. Other fields include genomics, chemistry and its applications, physics and parts of mathematics, the geo-sciences and earth monitoring, aerospace, pharmaceutics and other areas.

Some larger HBOs operate a significant number of international activities and linkages, including exchange arrangements and double degrees, and several would like a greater freedom to engage in entrepreneurial ventures abroad. These international activities tend to operate at the margins of programmes and the review team saw no evidence of an impact in organizational cultures. Perhaps the relatively low level of research activity in HBOs inhibits a transformative international engagement. Cross-border teaching can be decoupled from domestic teaching, but cross-border research rests on a domestically grounded research capacity and cannot be so separated.

The growing emphasis on university rankings, particularly the annual Shanghai Jiao Tong University ranking, is leading many countries and universities to focus on acquiring the personnel who drive improved performance in the ranking index, notably Thomson/ISI-classified 'HiCi' researchers and Nobel Prize winners. This has generated intensified global competition at the peak of the researcher labour market, a competition affected by relative salaries, conditions of work and research infrastructure and opportunities (Marginson and van der Wende, 2007). In addition, in future the Netherlands and many other nations are likely to face shortages of researchers and university faculty, given the present demographic 'bulge' of staff aged over 50 years.

In the longer term China and India will be the principal sources of globally mobile faculty and researchers. Knowledge industries in these nations will be competitive not just on price but on quality. The USA has proven to be a welcoming and effective recruiter of students and faculties from these countries, and other nations are smoothing the pathways to entry. It is likely that the Netherlands will be placed at a serious competitive disadvantage unless the problem of immigration blockages is resolved, and also unless a more enthusiastic attitude develops in relation to recruitment from Asia.

During the period of the country visit in April/May 2006 the review team was informed that previous bottlenecks in the migration pathways of high skilled knowledge workers had been opened up by regulatory changes to visa requirements so as to make the Netherlands more attractive to foreign academic personnel. It was noted that the Innovation Platform had been the vehicle for the policy change through its report on *Borderless mobility for knowledge migrants: how can we get talent to come to the Netherlands* (OCW, 2006e). On 1 October, 2004 a new 'fast-track' procedure was introduced whereby all prospective knowledge migrants deal with just one government authority and are issued the same type of permit. This fast track procedure did not initially cover foreign students and graduates, but it has since been modified to apply to foreign students (OCW, 2006d, p. 19).

Nevertheless it appears that the changes made so far have not been far-reaching enough to overcome the problem either in relation to foreign students or foreign faculty. Policy practice continues to be primarily dictated by a nationally protectionist outlook and the modus operandi of immigration authorities, rather than by the more global and innovation-oriented perspectives of universities and research networks. The difficulty of turning student status into permanent immigration status inhibits the potential of Dutch institutions to recruit both foreign students and faculty, especially from non-European countries.[15]

The 2006 OECD economic survey of the Netherlands emphasized the need for reforms 'to facilitate immigration of knowledge workers further by introducing a points system for immigrants, as in Canada, Australia and New Zealand, and by relaxing work permit rules' to permit foreign PHD students to stay on after graduation (p. 127). The issues are widely acknowledged within the Netherlands itself. During the visits of the review team to research agencies the comment was made several times that significant sectors of the Dutch population were not aware of the pressures of international competition and their manifestations in education and research. The Background Report (p. 89) also alludes to these problems. Rather than improvement; visa processing times are often uncompetitive vis-à-vis the UK; etc.

Cases cited to members of the review team suggest that in some cases at least foreign faculty and doctoral students of importance have been denied entry on the basis of judgments grounded less in the specific case than in general formulae based on country of origin. Some in government in the Netherlands evidence concerns that opening the door to high skill migrants will mean admitting their dependent family members. This is an example of exactly the wrong approach to the global knowledge economy. It is unrealistic to attempt to attract knowledge workers while dividing them from their dependents. If the Netherlands intends to provide a secure long term home for people of talent from around the world, then it needs to compete more effectively as the provider of a suitable living environment for their families.

---

[15] During a 10-day research programme in September 2006 in one of the leading research intensive universities, a programme conducted by one member of the review team but separate from and five months subsequent to the visits for the purposes of the review, the view was put by university executive and research leaders that immigration blockages were the principal factor inhibiting the global competitiveness of Dutch research universities. This area of policy was seen as the most in need of change, even more so than funding which normally occupies the principal attention in university discussion of government policy.

9.2 Strengths

In the Netherlands institutions are internationally minded. The importance of the worldwide environment is acknowledged and this is central to Dutch culture.

There is a formal policy commitment to opening up institutions to greater participation by foreign students and to increasing revenues from this source; and institutions have a growing financial incentive to increase foreign student recruitment. In the 2006-2007 academic year there were 1 200 English-language programmes at all levels. The 1 May 2006 adoption of a 'Code of conduct regarding international students in the Netherlands' commits signatory institutions to providing adequate information to international students in relations to programmes, fees, housing and other issues that in the past have been the cause of complaint (information from the Observatory on Borderless Education, 2006).

The Netherlands constitutes a relatively safe, secure and often attractive living environment, with excellent urban transport, in which the principal global language, English, is widely used. The Dutch fee structure is relatively competitive, for example in comparison with UK costs for foreign students. There are some working opportunities for foreign students.

The research universities are relatively strong in academic capacity and achievement and in that respect capable of attracting foreign faculty and high quality foreign doctoral students, providing the incentives and the regulatory environment are favourable. They have some of the conditions necessary to compete strongly for mobile labour in the more competitive global environment now emerging.

9.3 Weaknesses

There is no systematic monitoring at departmental level of the patterns of entry of foreign doctoral students, post-doctoral scholars and other faculty.

Departmental commitment to promoting and administrating foreign student entry is relatively weak compared to competitor countries, notably the UK. Though there is some interest in raising monies from international student fees, there is no evidence that internationalization of the student body is a high priority for agencies of government whether for revenue raising reasons or for other reasons.

While there is some commitment at institutional level, it is our impression based upon working experience in leading nations in international student recruitment - such as the US, UK, and Australia - that there is not yet in the Netherlands a similar environment and culture that favours the promotion of foreign student recruitment, retention and success.

The scope for foreign student recruitment is limited by the use of Dutch as the language of instruction in first degrees; and by the weight of the HBOs within Dutch higher education, because all else equal, a professional HBO degree, with its strong focus on local employment is less attractive than a research university degree from other nations.

The machinery for assessing and recognizing foreign universities and student qualifications is cumbersome. The slow development of cross-border cooperation in quality assurance is one inhibiting factor here.

Migration opportunities are a key driver of internationalization, in relation to both students and faculty. In the USA, UK and Australia short-term student migration often becomes long term or permanent settlement. In this respect the Netherlands provides a less attractive potential home to academic personnel than do the English-language nations. Potential academic immigrants face higher official hurdles than in some other nations. Non-white students face more cultural barriers in the Netherlands than they should.

Some competitor countries and their higher education institutions place greater emphasis on the value of diversity and the benefits provided to the nation by the presence of foreign students and migrants.

Evidence provided to the review team indicated that the overall entry of foreign doctoral students, post-doctoral faculty and more senior faculty was somewhat inhibited by lack of opportunities to establish, and/or ease of establishing, both migration status and faculty careers. This is a case-by-case matter. Most such anecdotes concerned immigration delays affecting senior staff but some younger people are also affected. These factors retard the capacity of the Netherlands to compete for globally mobile intellectual labour, especially at the top end of the global market. Further, Netherlands salary scales and total remuneration are uncompetitive vis-à-vis the USA. In the absence of more flexible arrangements, again this decisively inhibits recruitment of the highest calibre faculty. There seems to be little concern about this problem.

There is no systematic monitoring at departmental level of the patterns of exit of Dutch citizens at PhD and post-doctoral stages, nor attention to return rates. 'There are … hardly any figures on the mobility of graduates'. Nevertheless, it is known that a large number of science and technology PhDs from the Netherlands are now working in the United States (Background Report, p. 25). There is no scheme in place for bringing back expatriates, which compares unfavourably with some other countries. While there is broad awareness of net 'brain drain' there is little evidence of urgency or forward thinking in relation to the issue.

Dutch universities are prevented from offering a full qualification on foreign soil. This prevents deeper forms of international engagement, such as stand-alone or partner-based campuses in other nations, which can also be used as platforms for other activities such as foreign student recruitment into the Netherlands, research collaboration, and links to foreign industry.

9.4 Recommendations

For the most part policy makers understand the challenges and are pointing institutions in the right direction but there are questions about priority and impetus. Incentives are not strong enough and machinery is often lacking. International affairs are too readily marginalized in national administration. There is a reluctance to lead the nation through (and if possible beyond) the present anxieties about immigration even of high skilled professional migrants, and these anxieties are inhibiting the global effectiveness of the tertiary education sector.

The quantitative and qualitative growth of international openness and engagement are essential, especially but not only in the research-intensive universities. Higher education is now globally referenced throughout the world, and both global cooperation and global competition are increasingly influential in shaping national systems and institutions (Marginson, 2006).

Much of this international engagement is and should be pursued at the institution level, and within institutions at the discipline level, particularly in leading research universities. It should not be over-regulated. It is important it becomes more transparent and is coordinated where appropriate within the framework of overall national and institutional strategies and priorities. Here the principal potentials for national policy lie in framework-building activities (quality assurance systems, benchmarking, research funding programmes, national programmes of doctoral scholarships for foreign students, etc.) coupled with strategic subsidies and other interventions that are designed to stimulate particular initiatives and remove blockages.

Considerations of global strategy now take in relationships with other institutions within Europe, relationships through Europe with the rest of the world, and the 'stand-alone' relationships of individual universities and of Dutch education with the rest of the world. In this regard Dutch institutions can lead within Europe, for example by continuing to develop formal cross-border alliances and consortia such as the League of European Research Universities. It is in the interests of higher education in the Netherlands to support the development of a European-wide classification system in which the strengths of Dutch institutions will become more visible.

International panel members should be routinely included in programme accreditation and in research performance evaluation by institutions and disciplines. Global sensibilities and engagement can be systematized by regular benchmarking against Europe and the entire world, on the basis of discipline and the entire institution. It is important to develop more sophisticated and complex instruments for global comparison than those utilized by the existing systems of global university rankings. Special attention needs to be given to devising methods of cross-border benchmarking of HBOs with comparable institutions.

Internationalisation strategies in relation to personnel movement are unlikely to operate on the same scale, generate the same levels of income, or act as medium for the internal transformation of university culture, as has been evident in the UK and Australia. Because the prospects for fully commercial development are limited, internationalisation will need to be funded to a greater degree than in those nations. As in the USA, much of it will be dominated by subsidized research relationships rather than by revenue-raising.

The outward looking engagement of Dutch institutions in Europe and elsewhere provides the starting point for more balanced two-way flows of people and ideas than is the case in the English-speaking nations.

The fuller and more consistent opening of migration opportunities to high skill knowledge workers would assist internationalisation goals and supplement faculty quality in both HBOs and research universities, providing that faculty career opportunities are expanded. The labour market in science is a global one. Given the intrinsic excellence of Dutch research and scholarship coupled with the reputations and traditions of the leading universities, the Netherlands can aspire to a national R&D base capable not only of retaining local talent but attracting foreign and foreign-trained researcher talent, and providing a magnet capable of attracting not just Dutch multinational companies but foreign companies. Special attention needs to be given to potential recruits from Asian nations given their demographic weight, the rapidly developing research capacity of these nations, and the potential global mobility of their personnel. Half of all cross-border students, ands the overwhelming majority outside Europe, are from East Asia, Southeast Asia and South Asia. (In thinking about internationalisation it is important to distinguish between these zones and Mediterranean Asia in the Middle East). While seven of the government's ten priority countries for recruitment are from Asia - China, Taiwan, India, Indonesia, Thailand, Vietnam and Malaysia - in the institutions a sense of

Asian presence is not as strong as in the English-speaking countries or Germany. It would be a mistake to leave implementation of the official priority largely to higher education institutions.

The foreign student market continues to grow, increasing from 1.2 million students worldwide in 1990 to 2.7 million in 2004 (OECD, 2004d, p. 287). A modest expansion of international revenues is a realistic goal, focused in areas where Dutch education is relatively strong. Goals for foreign student recruitment should be less open-ended and more limited than hitherto, but pursued with greater vigour and consistency at departmental and institutional levels.

The Netherlands should target the quality end of the cross-border higher education market, not the mass high volume end; partly so as to use foreign recruitment to promote the knowledge economy credentials of the Netherlands and its higher education institutions. This suggests that the main avenue for recruitment should be academic Masters and doctoral programmes. There is some scope also for recruitment into English language professional Masters programmes in selected industries in both research universities and HBOs. In addition the number of Bachelor-level programmes in English should be increased.

Broadly the Ministry has adopted this set of priorities already. It is realistic and is on the right track but needs to lift the status of internationalisation within its own operation and to pursue policy objectives related to internationalisation more systematically, including promotional activities on behalf of Dutch tertiary education. The Background Report notes that 'apart from actually being world top, establishing a reputation as a leading and therefore interesting nation is terms of education and research is equally important' (p. 88). Government could do more to use diplomatic missions abroad to facilitate promotion and foreign student entry, and to showcase Dutch research achievements and the potential for collaboration. Web presence is also important.

Potentials for jointly badged degrees offered in collaboration with comparable foreign institutions, and the 'twinning' of programmes with foreign institutions in which the first part of the degree is provided outside the Netherlands could be further explored. Dutch institutions should be permitted to operate offshore campuses, provided that these campuses and their programmes are fully subject to national accreditation and quality assurance requirements.

Foreign providers operating on Netherlands soil should be included within the framework of national accreditation and quality assurance.

10. Conclusions

The Netherlands must strengthen the capacity of its tertiary system, rendering it more responsive and flexible, for a more European and global future, and more fully suited to integrating first and second generation immigrant populations into the human capital and culture of the nation.

The national system has great strengths in the face of these considerable challenges. It is well understood by its practitioners, professionalism is established at all levels, and quality assurance processes are functional. Both the research-intensive universities and the HBOs are intrinsically healthy, with viable traditions, competent personnel and 'thick' and active connection to the society and economy they serve. Both the HBO and the research university sector could be expanded to meet growing domestic and/or foreign demand. The research-intensive universities are strong in basic research, the bedrock of any research university system. More through their own voluntary evolution than through the system of national policies, mechanisms and incentives, some Dutch universities are not far below the level of the best universities in the world and have the potential to attract foreign students, faculty and international corporate investment in R&D when the right incentives are in place. The HBOs have a deep practical commitment to serving communities and industry and to bringing education and work closer together. In general, institutional leadership and management are competent and in the research universities there is a manifest ethos of self-regulated productivity and a widespread and genuine culture of research excellence.

However, for reasons outlined in Chapter Three, Dutch tertiary education is relatively weak in national priority setting, in the identification of emerging problems; and the long-term approach to policy. This inhibits an effective response to the global challenges and to the more culturally diverse resident population with its special educational needs. The national personality of the system is poorly developed. The OCW seems to have insufficient capacity either to steer the tertiary education system in a focused manner, for example by developing new instruments of funding and governance. Coordination with the economic departments of government is insufficient. Internal departmental coherence is insufficient. By comparison short-term responses to political guidance are well developed.

In our view the key challenges facing the system in the immediate and near-term future include:

- The slow rate of growth of public and private investment in higher education and research, compared to most other OECD countries, and decline in the GDP share;

- The slow rate of improvement in participation levels and some decline in the global competitiveness of Dutch higher education in relation to this indicator;

- The need to lift educational and social achievement among immigrant 'non-Western' populations;

- The need to develop student selection and student choice-making as policy instruments; and to devise a more effective student-institution relationship than that constituted by automatic entry, ballots, enrolment over capacity levels, and end of year one selection on the basis of failure;

- The need to develop mechanisms that will focus effectively on improving excellence in teaching;

- The potential of institutional diversity within the traditional sectors and across barriers such as WO/HBO, public/private and local/foreign; the need to develop a more flexible and needs-driven binary system; the need for greater variation in programmes on the basis of time length and price; and the strategic question of whether and how the Netherlands might develop more globally competitive research universities;

- The need to establish a framework of conditions and incentives that will attract foreign students (especially doctoral students) and faculty of high quality, both to augment the Dutch knowledge economy in the present and provide part of the basic human infrastructure in the future, given the ageing of the academic population and the problem of 'brain drain' to the USA.

The positive message here is that there is very considerable scope, in both national government and institutional leadership and management, to develop new instruments of government that could enable a more strategic approach to resource distribution and priority setting.

In national policy on research and innovation there are too many programmes and mechanisms, and the element of direct competition for research support should be enhanced. However, there are also high quality agencies and programmes (see Chapter Seven). Substantial efforts have been made to connect industry and university research. Here the continuing 'Dutch paradox' owes itself not so much to weaknesses in innovation policy as to the difficulty of the task. Much can be achieved by resetting incentives and activities on the supply side, for example so as to attracting more foreign R&D investment. But the level of business R&D in the Netherlands also depends on the demand side (OECD, 2006b, p. 18). It is partly a function of industry structure, including the small number of major corporate players, and the relatively small size of the high-tech sector within the economy.

Perhaps the major R&D players in the corporate sector could do more to encourage utilisation in Dutch universities and institutes and foster a flourishing SME subcontractor network. The review team would need more time to thoroughly investigate this aspect. But we note that there may be scope for a more active policy here. Dutch government support for major Dutch multinationals might more strongly encourage corporations to cooperate with Dutch nodes of the global knowledge economy. At the same time, in the longer term it is likely that the research and innovation system will have a greater scope to expand its role in serving European and global business than its role in serving Dutch business alone. This raises questions of the identity of policy – European? Dutch? a combination? – that are fascinating in themselves, but beyond the competence of this review to address.

There might be more scope for expanding university-private sector links among emerging knowledge-intensive companies than large companies. Here, though 'the Netherlands also has a relatively small share of high-tech and medium high-tech sectors in the total economy' (OCW, 2004a, p. 95).

A downside of the 'Dutch paradox' is that this difficult policy problem has captured a great deal of governmental energy while other issues have been ignored. In policy debate certain issues can take on symbolic importance that moves beyond the content of the issues themselves. Debates become rituals enabling key actors to make public noises that position themselves in expected ways, rather than giving consideration to different practical solutions. The same kind of comment could be made about the tensions on the binary line, and the public debates associated with these. Perhaps less important than whether the HBOs provide funded Arts degrees and expand research activities are the reforms necessary to modernise their administrative systems, improve staff qualifications and render them internationally competitive and attractive. The 'Dutch paradox' and the binary line can also distract attention from underlying problems of the system, problems that are perhaps more obvious to outsiders than insiders.

The flip side of a stable higher education system with vital traditions is that change is more likely to occur through evolution than revolution. The review team finds that the intrinsic culture of higher education in the Netherlands embodies certain fundamental weaknesses but it will take some time for these issues to be overcome or even to be effectively addressed, because they are deeply rooted.

One entrenched problem is the national habit of treating higher education as exclusively a young person's preserve. Another and even more fundamental problem is the tendency to manage diversity through segmentation and path dependence; rather than through pluralism, mobility and multiple opportunities within common systems. For a review team from outside the Netherlands this aspect was disturbing.

The segmentation of the school age population leads to neatly functioning educational progressions, especially for students in the academic stream. It also allows high quality to be secured in the academic stream at moderate overall cost, constituting the 'value for money' referred to in the Ministry's Background Report. But there are many thousands of other students who might have benefit from an academic education who are streamed away from it at an early age, and do not find their way back. Because of limited opportunities to track upwards and the absence of an infrastructure for lifelong learning at scale there are few second chances. Of considerable concern are the relatively high presence of immigrant families in the bottom stream at school, and the relatively low rates of completion among students from the same families in higher education. There is a real danger that education is entrenching serious social divisions along cultural lines.

But there is also a positive opportunity here. Higher education could play the key role in integrating immigrant communities more effectively into Dutch society: by providing an equitable framework of opportunity, by sustaining and respecting cultural diversity in the classroom and outside it, and by practising tolerance and respect for religious freedoms.

In general the tertiary system is not sufficiently inclusive. Equity and pastoral considerations are important in Dutch policy but are more likely to be applied within the different segments and sectors, rather than between them and across the whole population. Aggregate participation goals seem to be less important in the Netherlands than in many other countries. There is insufficient urgency about the 50% target and moving beyond it. Perhaps it is assumed that the HBOs can simply be pumped up to fit without changing programmes while the universities should go on educating a small and selected part of the age group as they have always done. It is as if higher education has nothing much to contribute to half the population. It is salutary to compare Dutch levels of participation in higher education with such nations as Canada and Korea. Is academic ability more broadly distributed in those countries than in the Netherlands? We think this unlikely, given the high level of performance Dutch youth demonstrate in the PISA assessment.

Another example of the tendency to handle diversity via segmentation and hierarchy, rather than inclusion and universality, is the present configuration of institutional diversity. Rather than encouraging a broad range of horizontal diversity the system has been managed in terms of a firm binary line (again, difference is expressed hierarchically) with problems of boundary policing, plus uniformity within each separate sector. There is nothing wrong with the binary principle but this is not the only possible form of diversity. Further, the instinctive preference for uniform systems inhibits experiment in modes of delivery and fee levels.

In the longer run it may be that the Netherlands will be better served by a single system of tertiary education with much more scope for variation in mission, programmes and modes of delivery, with individual missions grounded in government determined national need coupled with responsiveness to students, employers and localities. At the least it will be necessary to move towards greater flexibility and cross-sector collaboration, as in Finland. But the final resolution of these issues is a distant prospect at this stage. Meanwhile it is important to make the binary divide work – to meet the wider needs of the nation rather than the aspiration of any particular institution or sector - rather than it being continually eroded. The role of the WOs in basic research and doctoral training constitutes the essential dividing line between research-intensive institutions and HBOs.

There is the evident need to develop stronger data instruments in many strategic areas such as participation and success by ethnic group and by socio-economic status; the cross-border mobility of faculty and doctoral students moving in both directions; institutional revenues off budget, etc. It is said that 'an army marches on its stomach' – and it is equally true that a government department moves on the basis of data. It gains its policy edge from its capacity to imagine the system in complex sociological and economic terms, to predict outcomes, and to fashion well-understood options for government and institutions to consider.

10.1 Recommendation

To develop a sound framework for national policy, policymakers must have a deep understanding of the institutions for which they are setting policy - whether police departments, hospitals, or universities. The most reliable way of developing this understanding is through working experience and immersion in the institution itself. In many countries this is achieved by the recruitment of senior Ministry staff from higher education institutions, a practice that does not appear to take place in the Netherlands. We believe that OCW policymaking for higher education would be strengthened if its staff possessed a deepened understanding of and connectivity to higher education institutions. This can be accomplished through the recruitment of staff who have worked in tertiary institutions, devising plans of flexible secondment, even of a few months' duration, or by other means.

References

Advisory Council for Science and Technology (AWT) (2005), *Paying for an Asset: Funding University Research,* Report 61, at www.awt.nl/uploads/files/a61uk.pdf

Bureau for Economic Policy Analysis (CPB) (2005), *Scarcity of Science and Engineering Graduates in the Netherlands,* CPB Document No. 92.

Canton E. (2001), "Should Tuition Fees Be Increased?", Bureau for Economic Policy Analysis *(*CPB).

Centre for Higher Education Policy Studies (CHEPS) (2005), *Myths and Methods on Access and Participation in Higher Education in International Comparison,* University of Twente.

Centre for Higher Education Policy Studies (CHEPS) (2006), *CHEPS Unplugged,* University of Twente, Vol. 6 (1).

ECABO (Centre of Expertise on Vocational Education, Training and Labour) (2006), *Monitor arbeidsmarkt beroepsonderweis in 2006-2007* at: http://loket2.r-i.nl/media/items6/122.pdf

Enders J. and de Weert (2004), "Science, Training and Career", in Higher Education Policy, Vol. 17, June 2004, pp. 129-133.

Fuente, A. de la and J.F. Jimeno (2005), "The Private and Fiscal returns to Schooling and the Effect of Public Policies on Private Incentives to Invest in Education: A General Framework and Some Results for the EU", *CESifo Working Paper* No. 1392.

Groot, W. and E. Plug (1999), "Geen tekort aan technisch opgeleiden", *Economisch Statistische Berichten,* 4216, pp. 608-615.

Hartog, J., J. Odink and J. Smits (1999), "Private Returns to Education in the Netherlands", in R. Asplund, and P.T. Pereira, eds., *Returns to Human Capital in Europe,* Helsinki: ETLA, The Research Institute of the Finnish Economy.

Institute for Scientific Information (2006), http://isihighlycited.com

Marginson, S. (2006), 'Dynamics of national and global competition in higher education', *Higher Education*, 52, pp. 1-39.

Marginson, S. and M. van der Wende (2007), "Globalisation and Higher Education", *OECD Education Working Papers Series*, No. 8.

Ministry of Economic Affairs (2006), *Science, Technology and Innovation in the Netherlands: Policies, Facts and Figures, 2006.*

Ministry of Education, Culture and Science (OCW) (2004a), *Science, Technology and Innovation in the Netherlands: Policies, facts and figures*, 2004.

Ministry of Education, Culture and Science (OCW) (2004b), *Onderwijs en Onderzoek Plan* (HOOP).

Ministry of Education, Culture and Science (OCW) (2005), *Kennis in Kaart*, 2005.

Ministry of Education, Culture and Science (OCW) (2006a), *Beleidsgerichte Studies Hoger onderwijs en Wetenschappelijk onderzoek 2006, nr. 124*, Jos de Jonge and Jurriaan Berger, OECD Thematic Review of Tertiary Education, The Netherlands.

Ministry of Education, Culture and Science (OCW) (2006b), *Key Figures 2000-2004: Education, Culture And Science In The Netherlands.*

Ministry of Education, Culture and Science (OCW) (2006c), *Kennis in Kaart, 2006.*

Ministry of Education, Culture and Science (OCW) (2006d), *Making the Most of Talented Researchers.*

Ministry of Education, Culture and Science (OCW) (2006e), *Borderless Mobility for Knowledge Migrants: How Can We Get Talent To Come To The Netherlands?* www.minocw.nl/documenten/Researchtalent.pdf

Nederlands Vlaamse Accreditatie Organisatie (NVAO) (2005), *Bridging the Gap Between Theory and Practice: Possible Degrees for a Binary System.*

Netherlands Observatory of Science and Technology (NOWT) (2005), *Science and Technology Indicators, Summary,* 2005.

OECD (2003), *Public-private Partnerships for Research and Innovation: An evaluation of the Dutch experience.* Paris: OECD.

OECD (2004a), *OECD Thematic Review of Tertiary Education: Guidelines for Country Participation in the Review*, OECD, Paris (available from www.oecd.org/edu/tertiary/review).

OECD (2004b), *Science, technology and Innovation in the Netherlands, 2004*, Paris, OECD.

OECD (2004c), *Science, Technology and Industry Outlook 2004*, Paris, OECD.

OECD (2004d), *Education at a Glance, OECD Indicators 2004*, Paris, OECD.

OECD (2005a), *Education at a Glance, OECD Indicators 2005*, Paris, OECD.

OECD (2005b), *Making Better Use of Knowledge Creation in Innovation Activities*, Paris, OECD.

OECD (2006a), *Education at a Glance, OECD Indicators 2006*, Paris, OECD.

OECD (2006b), *Economic Surveys, Netherlands*, Paris, OECD.

OECD (2006c), *Where Immigrant Students Succeed: A Comparative Review of Performance and Engagement in PISA 2003*, Paris, OECD.

Shanghai Jiao Tong University Institute of Higher Education (2006), *Academic Ranking Of World Universities* http://ed.sjtu.edu.cn/ranking.htm

Sonneveld, H. and H. Oost (2006), *Foreign Peer Reviewers about the Quality and Added Value of Dutch Research Schools.*

Stichting de Beauvoir (2006), in Samenwerking met de VSNU, *Monitor Vrouwelijke Hoogleraren 2006*, at www.stichtingdebeauvoir.nl

van Steen, J., P. Donselaar and I. Schrijvers (eds.) (2004 and 2006), *Science, Technology and Innovation in the Netherlands: Policies, facts and figures*, Ministries of OCW (Education, Science and Culture) and EZ (Economic Affairs), The Hague.

Witte, J. (2006), *Change of Degrees and Degrees of Change: Comparing Adaptations of European Higher Education Systems in the Context of the Bologna Process*, doctoral dissertation, Centre for Higher Education Policy Studies, University of Twente.

Appendix 1: The OECD Review Team

Nicola Channon is Head of Operations, Institutional Review at the Quality Assurance Agency for Higher Education for the United Kingdom (QAA), a post she took up in 1998, after serving as Head of Quality Assurance at the Scottish Qualifications Authority (SQA).

Terttu Luukkonen is a Head of Unit at the Research Institute of the Finnish Economy, where she has worked since 2001. She has previously held positions with the Technical Research Centre of Finland (Chief Research Scientist, Director of VTT Group for Technology Studies, 1995-2001) and the Academy of Finland, the funding body for high-quality scientific research, largely conducted in universities (1974-1995).

Simon Marginson has been Professor of Higher Education in the Centre for the Study of Higher Education at the University of Melbourne in Australia since 2006. He was previously Professor at Monash University in Melbourne and Director of the Monash Centre for Research in International Education (2000-2006). He is an Australian Professorial Fellow and Fellow of the Academy of Social Sciences, Australia. He served as rapporteur.

Jon Oberg has served the US state of Nebraska as Director of the State Office of Planning and Programming and as its Chief State Fiscal Officer; has was formerly the president of a state association representing private colleges and universities; the legislative director for the United States Senator for Nebraska; and served in the US Institute of Education Sciences, with responsibility for policy analysis and evaluation.

Thomas Weko, Analyst, Education and Training Policy Division, Directorate for Education, OECD.

Appendix 2: National Co-ordinator and Authors of the Country Background Report

National Co-ordinator for the Netherlands

The national coordinator for the review was Marlies Leegwater senior policy advisor at the Ministry of Education, Culture, and Science, Directorate for Higher Education.

Country Background Report Authors

Jos de Jonge and Jurriaan Berger of the firm EIM authored the Country Background Report for the Ministry of Culture, and Science (OCW), published October 2006 as Beleidsgerichte studies Hoger Onderwijs en Wetenschappelijk onderzoek No. 124; OECD Thematic Review of Tertiary Education, The Netherlands.

Appendix 3: Programme of the Review Visit

Monday, April 24

Morning: Ministry of Education (OCW)
13.00 – 14.00   Innovation Platform
14.00 – 15.00   Ministry of Economic Affairs
15.00 – 16.00   Ministry of Finance
16.30 – 18.30   HBO-Raad

Tuesday, April 25

9.30 – 11.00   VNO-NCW (Confederation of industry and employers, Standing
                 Committee on higher education)
12.30 – 14.00   Aob Utrecht
14.00 – 15.30   TNO, Delft
16.00 – 17.30   NVAO Den Haag

Wednesday, April 26

8.30 – 10.00   Inspectorate for Higher Education, OCW
9.30 – 12.00   NWO (Research Council) and AWT (Advisory Council for Science
                 and Technology)
13.30 – 15.00   VSNU (Association of Universities)
15.30   ISO and LSVB-student organisations

Thursday, April 27

8.30 – 10.00   Hogeschool InHolland Den Haag (central management)
10.30 – 11.30   HBO-ICT academie Zoetermeer
11.30 – 12.30   Mr. Chang, Chair of Chang Commission
12.00 – 16.00   Haagse Hogeschool

Friday, April 28

10.00 – 12.30	University of Utrecht
14.00 – 18.00	Tilburg Fontys and Avans hogeschool s'Hertogenbosch

Monday, May 1

9.00 – 10.00	TU Delft
10.00 – 12.00	Hogeschool voor mode management
13.00 – 15.00	InHolland Den Haag
13.30 – 15.00	Free University Amsterdam
16.00 – 17.30	Hobeon Den Haag

Tuesday, May 2

8.30 – 9.30	Technical University Delft
10.00 – 12.00	MKB Nederland
13.00 – 14.30	Briefing OCW

Appendix 4: Comparative Indicators on Tertiary Education

	Netherlands	OECD mean	Netherlands' rank[1]	% to OECD mean[2]
OUTCOMES				
% of the population aged 25-64 with tertiary qualifications (2004)				
Tertiary-type B – Total	2	9	22/24	22
Males	3		22/23	-
Females	2		21/25	-
Tertiary-type A– Total	26	19[i]	3/30	137
Males	28		3/30	-
Females	24		4/30	-
Advanced research programmes – Total	-		-	-
Males	1		-	-
Females	-		-	-
% of the population aged 25-34 with tertiary qualifications (2004)				
Tertiary-type B	2	11	22/24	18
Tertiary-type A and advanced research programmes	32	24	2/24	133
% of the population aged 55-64 with tertiary qualifications (2004)				
Tertiary-type B	2	6	13/24	33
Tertiary-type A and advanced research programmes	22	13	2/24	169
% of the population aged 25-64 with tertiary qualifications – time trends				
1991	20	18	11/21	111
2004	29	25	11/30	116
% of the population aged 25-34 with tertiary qualifications – time trends				
1991	22	20	9/21	110
2004	34	31	14/30	110

	Netherlands	OECD mean	Netherlands' rank[1]	% to OECD mean[2]
Average years in formal education (2004)[3]	11.2	11.9	23/30	94
Survival rates in tertiary education (2004)				
Number of graduates divided by the number of new entrants in the typical year of entrance				
Tertiary-type A education	76	70	6/21	109
Tertiary-type B education	-	62	-	-
Advanced research programmes	-	67	-	-
Average duration of tertiary studies (in years) (year varies)[4]				
All tertiary education	-	3.94	-	-
Tertiary-type B education	-	2.38	-	-
Tertiary-type A and advanced research programmes	5.24	4.42	7/24	119
Tertiary graduates by field of study[5] (2002)				
Tertiary-type A				
Education	18.2	-	7/27	
Humanities and arts	6.5	-	23/27	
Social sciences, business and law	34.9	-	13/27	
Science	5.1	-	24/27	
Engineering, manufacturing and construction	10.5	-	17/27	
Agriculture	2.1	-	12/27	
Health and welfare	20.3	-	5/27	
Services	2.4	-	15/27	
Not known or unspecified	-	-	-	
All fields	100	-	-	
Tertiary-type B				
Education	-	-	-	
Humanities and arts	-	-	-	
Social sciences, business and law	-	-	-	
Science	-	-	-	
Engineering, manufacturing and construction	-	-	-	
Agriculture	-	-	-	
Health and welfare	-	-	-	
Services	-	-	-	
Not known or unspecified	-	-	-	
All fields	-	-	-	

	Netherlands	OECD mean	Netherlands' rank[1]	% to OECD mean[2]
Advanced research programmes				
Education	-	-	-	
Humanities and arts	8.7	-	23/27	
Social sciences, business and law	17.2	-	12/26	
Science	19.6	-	8/27	
Engineering, manufacturing and construction	17.5	-	9/26	
Agriculture	8.5	-	7/26	
Health and welfare	28.4	-	5/27	
Services	-	-	-	
Not known or unspecified	-	-	-	
All fields	-	-	-	
Tertiary graduates by field of study[5] per 10 000 population (2002)				
Tertiary-type A				
Education	9.73	-	7/27	
Humanities and arts	3.47	-	2/27	
Social sciences, business and law	18.70	-	10/27	
Science	2.75	-	2/27	
Engineering, manufacturing and construction	5.64	-	16/27	
Agriculture	1.11	-	10/27	
Health and welfare	10.88	-	7/27	
Services	1.27	-	14/27	
Not known or unspecified	-	-	-	
All fields	53.58	-	15/27	
Tertiary-type B				
Education	-	-	-	
Humanities and arts	-	-	-	
Social sciences, business and law	-	-	-	
Science	-	-	-	
Engineering, manufacturing and construction	-	-	-	
Agriculture	-	-	-	
Health and welfare	-	-	-	
Services	-	-	-	
Not known or unspecified	-	-	-	
All fields	-	-	-	

OECD REVIEWS OF TERTIARY EDUCATION – NETHERLANDS – ISBN 978-92-64-03925-4 – © OECD 2008

	Netherlands	OECD mean	Netherlands' rank[1]	% to OECD mean[2]
Advanced research programmes				
Education	-	-	-	
Humanities and arts	0.14	-	19/27	
Social sciences, business and law	0.27	-	13/26	
Science	0.31	-	18/27	
Engineering, manufacturing and construction	0.28	-	10/26	
Agriculture	0.14	-	6/26	
Health and welfare	0.45	-	6/27	
Services	-	-	-	
Not known or unspecified	-	-	-	
All fields	1.60	-	12/27	
Employment ratio and educational attainment[6] (2004)				
Number of 25 to 64-year-olds in employment as a percentage of the population aged 25 to 64				
Lower secondary education				
Males	79.6	72.1	9/30	110
Females	51.5	48.9	13/30	105
Upper secondary education (ISCED 3A)				
Males	86.5	81.6	6/29	106
Females	73.9	65.3	6/29	113
Post-secondary non-tertiary education				
Males	-	-	-	
Females	-	-	-	
Tertiary education, type B				
Males	85.4	87.6	20/26	97
Females	74.5	77.2	10/26	97
Tertiary education, type A and advanced research programmes				
Males	88.7	89.1	17/30	100
Females	75.8	79.1	17/30	96

	Netherlands	OECD mean	Netherlands' rank[1]	% to OECD mean[2]
Employment ratio and educational attainment (2004)				
Number of 30 to 34-year-olds in employment as a percentage				
Lower secondary education				
Males	88.1	80.2	6/22	110
Females	60.6	51.2	5/22	118
Upper secondary education (ISCED 3A)				
Males	-	87.0	-	-
Females	-	167.8	-	-
Post-secondary non-tertiary education				
Males	-	89.3	-	-
Females	-	75.9	-	-
Tertiary education, type B				
Males	95.5	93.4	9/23	102
Females	96.8	78.5	16/23	123
Tertiary education, type A and advanced research programmes				
Males	95.5	93.6	5/23	102
Females	89.7	82.1	2/23	109
Unemployment ratio and educational attainment[7] (2004)				
Number of 25 to 64-year-olds who are unemployed as a percentage of the population aged 25 to 64				
Lower secondary education				
Males	5.8	10.1	18/29	57
Females	4.4	11.0	25/29	40
Upper secondary education (ISCED 3A)				
Males	3.8	5.7	22/28	67
Females	3.7	7.2	23/28	51
Post-secondary non-tertiary education				
Males	4.2	-	6/17	-
Females	2.7	-	14/17	-
Tertiary education, type B				
Males	2.6	3.7	20/25	70
Females	4.6	4.5	9/24	102
Tertiary education, type A and advanced research programmes[ii]				
Males	2.5	3.5	20/29	71
Females	2.9	4.3	19/29	67

	Netherlands	OECD mean	Netherlands' rank[1]	% to OECD mean[2]
Unemployment ratio and educational attainment (2004)				
Number of 30 to 34-year-olds who are unemployed as a percentage				
Lower secondary education				
Males	6.0	11.1	18/22	54
Females	8.8	15.2	14/22	58
Upper secondary education (ISCED 3A)				
Males	-	6.2	-	-
Females	-	8.7	-	-
Post-secondary non-tertiary education				
Males	-	8.1	-	-
Females	-	6.8	-	-
Tertiary education, type B				
Males	2.9	4.5	15/23	64
Females	3.2	5.4	15/23	59
Tertiary education, type A and advanced research programmes[ii]				
Males	2.6	3.4	15/23	76
Females	2.1	5.1	21/23	41
Ratio of the population not in the labour force and educational attainment (2004)				
Number of 25 to 64-year-olds not in the labour force as a percentage of the population aged 25 to 64				
Lower secondary education				
Males	16.6	20.0	12/22	83
Females	45.3	45.4	13/22	100
Upper secondary education (ISCED 3A)				
Males	-	14.5	-	-
Females	-	30.1	-	-
Post-secondary non-tertiary education				
Males	-	9.7	-	-
Females	-	22.7	-	-
Tertiary education, type B				
Males	10.3	8.9	9/24	116
Females	20.7	18.6	6/24	111
Tertiary education, type A and advanced research programmes				
Males	9.0	7.7	5/23	117
Females	7.8	15.2	13/23	51

	Netherlands	OECD mean	Netherlands' rank[1]	% to OECD mean[2]
Ratio of the population not in the labour force and educational attainment (2004) Number of 30 to 34-year-olds not in the labour force as a percentage of the population aged 30 to 34 Lower secondary education				
Males	6.3	10.1	14/22	62
Females	35.5	39.9	14/22	89
Upper secondary education (ISCED 3A)				
Males	-	7.3	-	-
Females	-	25.9	-	-
Post-secondary non-tertiary education				
Males	-	2.8	-	-
Females	-	18.3	-	-
Tertiary education, type B				
Males	4.0	3.2	8/23	125
Females	20.7	16.9	5/23	122
Tertiary education, type A and advanced research programmes				
Males	2.1	3.5	9/23	60
Females	8.4	13.5	21/23	62
Earnings of tertiary graduates aged 25-64 relative to upper secondary graduates aged 25-64 (2002) (upper secondary = 100)				
All tertiary	148	-	-	-
Earnings of tertiary graduates aged 30-44 relative to upper secondary graduates aged 30-44 (2002) (upper secondary = 100)				
All tertiary	147	-	-	-
Trends in relative earnings of tertiary graduates aged 25-64 (upper secondary and post-secondary non-tertiary education = 100)				
1997	141	-	-	-
2002	148	-	-	-

	Netherlands	OECD mean	Netherlands' rank[1]	% to OECD mean[2]
PATTERNS OF PARTICIPATION				
Participation rates of all persons aged 15 and over by programme (2002)				
Per cent of all persons aged 15 and over in tertiary type-5A programmes	3.9	4.0	14/26	98
Per cent of all persons aged 15 and over in tertiary type-5B programmes	0.1	0.7	24/26	14
Per cent of all persons aged 15 and over in tertiary type-6 programmes	0	0.2	20/23	-
Per cent of all persons aged 15 and over in all tertiary programmes	4.0	4.9	18/26	82
Index of change in total tertiary enrolment (2004) (1995 = 100)				
Total				
Attributable to change in population[8]	-	96	-	
Attributable to change in enrolment rates[9]	-	151	-	
Enrolment rates (2004)				
Full-time and part-time students in public and private institutions, by age				
Students aged 15-19 as a percentage of the population aged 15-19	86.1	80.5	1/28	107
Students aged 20-29 as a percentage of the population aged 20-29	25.5	24.7	14/28	103
Students aged 30-39 as a percentage of the population aged 30-39	2.9	5.6	22/28	52
Students aged 40 and over as a percentage of the population aged 40 and over	0.8	1.6	12/22	50

	Netherlands	OECD mean	Netherlands' rank[1]	% to OECD mean[2]
Age distribution of enrolments (2003)				
Persons aged 35 and over as a per cent of all enrolments in tertiary type-5A programmes	9.1	10.3	11/24	88
Persons aged 35 and over as a per cent of all enrolments in tertiary type-5B programmes	25.7	16.2	6/21	159
Persons aged 35 and over as a per cent of all enrolments in tertiary type-6 programmes	4.4	30.2	21/22	15
Persons aged 35 and over as a per cent of all enrolments in total tertiary programmes	9.3	11.7	11/24	79
Persons aged less than 25 as a per cent of all enrolments in tertiary type-5A programmes	71.4	63.9	8/26	112
Persons aged less than 25 as a per cent of all enrolments in tertiary type-5B programmes	45.4	58.9	19/26	77
Persons aged less than 25 as a per cent of all enrolments in tertiary type-6 programmes	14.5	10.2	7/21	142
Persons aged less than 25 as a per cent of all enrolments in total tertiary programmes	70.4	61.5	9/27	114
Persons aged less than 20 as a per cent of all enrolments in tertiary type-5A programmes	18.6	13.9	11/27	134
Persons aged less than 20 as a per cent of all enrolments in tertiary type-5B programmes	9.8	17.2	18/27	57
Persons aged less than 20 as a per cent of all enrolments in tertiary type-6 programmes	-	0.4	-	-
Persons aged less than 20 as a per cent of all enrolments in total tertiary programmes	18.2	15.0	12/27	121

	Netherlands	OECD mean	Netherlands' rank[1]	% to OECD mean[2]
Gender distribution of enrolments (2003)				
Females as a per cent of enrolments in tertiary type-5A programmes	51.0	53.2	21/29	96
Females as a per cent of enrolments in tertiary type-5B programmes	59.6	54.8	10/29	109
Females as a per cent of enrolments in tertiary type-6 programmes	41.0	44.0	21/28	93
Females as a per cent of total tertiary enrolments	51.0	33.2	21/29	154
Net entry rates into tertiary education[10] (2004)				
Tertiary-type B				
Total	-	16	-	-
Males	-	14	-	-
Females	-	16	-	-
Tertiary-type A				
Total	56	53	10/26	106
Males	52	48	10/25	108
Females	61	59	12/25	103
Distribution of students in tertiary education by type of institution[11] (2004)				
Tertiary-type B education, public	-	64.9	-	-
Tertiary-type B education, government-dependent private	-	19.1	-	-
Tertiary-type B education, independent private	-	13.4	-	-
Tertiary-type A and advanced research programmes, public	-	76.7	-	-
Tertiary-type A and advanced research programmes, government-dependent private	100	12.0	1/14	833
Tertiary-type A and advanced research programmes, independent private	-	11.7	-	-
Distribution of students in tertiary education by mode of study (2004)				
Tertiary-type B education				
Full-time	-	72.1	-	
Part-time	-	24.0	-	
Tertiary-type A and advanced research programmes				
Full-time	81.4	80.7	15/27	101
Part-time	18.6	19.3	13/20	96

	Netherlands	OECD mean	Netherlands' rank[1]	% to OECD mean[2]
Age distribution of net entrants into tertiary education, tertiary-type A (2004)				
Age at 20th percentile (20% of new entrants are below this age)	18.4	-	-	-
Age at 50th percentile (50% of new entrants are below this age)	19.8	-	-	-
Age at 80th percentile (80% of new entrants are below this age)	22.7	-	-	-
Foreign students as a percentage of all students (2003) (foreign and domestic students)[12]	3.9	7.4	15/27	53
Index of change in foreign students as a percentage of all students (2004) (foreign and domestic students) (2000 = 100)	152	161	11/28	94
National students enrolled abroad in other reporting countries relative to total tertiary enrolment[13] **(2003)**	0.9	4.0	27/29	23
Expected changes of the 20-29 age group by 2015 relative to 2005 (2005 = 100)[14]	109	97	6/30	112
Upper secondary attainment rates (2004) % of persons aged 25-34 with at least upper secondary education	80	77	16/30	104
Expected years of tertiary education under current conditions (2004) Full-time and part-time[15]	2.7	3.0	20/28	90
Admission to tertiary education[16] Source: Eurydice (2005) Limitation of the number of places available in most branches of public and grant-aided private tertiary education (2002/03)				
Limitation at national level with direct control of selection		1/35	-	-
Selection by institutions (In accordance with their capacity or national criteria)		23/35	-	-
Free access to most branches	√	11/35	-	-

	Netherlands	OECD mean	Netherlands' rank[1]	% to OECD mean[2]
EXPENDITURE				
Annual expenditure on tertiary education institutions per student, public and private institutions (2003) In equivalent US dollars converted using PPPs, based on full-time equivalents				
All tertiary education (including R&D activities)	13444	11254	3/19	107
Tertiary-type B education (including R&D activities)	-	-	-	-
Tertiary-type A and advanced research programmes (including R&D activities)	13537	-	-	-
All tertiary education excluding R&D activities	8337	8093	8/26	103
Annual expenditure on tertiary education institutions per student relative to GDP per capita, public and private institutions (2003) Based on full-time equivalents				
All tertiary education (including R&D activities)	42	43	9/28	98
Tertiary-type B education (including R&D activities)	-	30	-	-
Tertiary-type A and advanced research programmes (including R&D activities)	43	44	8/18	98
All tertiary education excluding R&D activities	26	33	20/26	79
Cumulative expenditure on educational institutions per student over the average duration of tertiary studies[17] (2003) In equivalent US dollars converted using PPPs				
All tertiary education	-	43030	-	-
Tertiary-type B education	-	-	-	-
Tertiary-type A and advanced research programmes	70932	-	-	-

	Netherlands	OECD mean	Netherlands' rank[1]	% to OECD mean[2]
Change in tertiary education expenditure per student relative to different factors				
Index of change between 1995 and 2003 (1995 = 100, 2003 constant prices)				
Change in expenditure	112	146	23/25	77
Change in the number of students	109	138	13/24	79
Change in expenditure per student	103	106	16/24	97
Change in tertiary education expenditure per student				
In equivalent US dollars converted using PPPs (2001 constant prices and 2001 constant PPPs)				
1995	12311	9284	5/22	133
2001	12974	10052	6/26	129
Expenditure on tertiary education institutions as a percentage of GDP, from public and private sources				
All tertiary education, 2003	1.3	1.4	18/29	93
Tertiary-type B education, 2003	-	0.2	-	-
Tertiary-type A education, 2003	1.3	1.2	8/18	108
All tertiary education, 1995	1.2	-	8/23	-
Relative proportions of public and private expenditure on educational institutions, for tertiary education				
Distribution of public and private sources of funds for educational institutions after transfers from public sources				
Public sources, 2003	78.6	76.4	16/28	103
Private sources, household expenditure, 2003	11.5	-	-	-
Private sources, expenditure of other private entities, 2003	9.9	-	-	-
Private sources, all private sources, 2003	21.4	23.6	13/28	91
Private sources, private, of which subsidised, 2003	1.5	1.5	7/12	100
Public sources, 1995	80.6	-	10/19	-
Private sources, household expenditure, 1995	10.1	-	9/15	-
Private sources, expenditure of other private entities, 1995	9.3	-	5/10	-
Private sources, all private sources, 1995	19.4	-	10/19	-
Private sources, private, of which subsidised, 1995	2.5	-	5/8	-

OECD REVIEWS OF TERTIARY EDUCATION – NETHERLANDS – ISBN 978-92-64-03925-4 – © OECD 2008

	Netherlands	OECD mean	Netherlands' rank[1]	% to OECD mean[2]
Distribution of total public expenditure on tertiary education (2003) Public expenditure on tertiary education transferred to educational institutions and public transfers to the private sector, as a percentage of total public expenditure on tertiary education				
Direct public expenditure on public institutions	-	71.7	-	-
Direct public expenditure on private institutions	74.1	11.2	2/21	662
Indirect public transfers and payments to the private sector	25.9	17.4	6/28	149
Expenditure on tertiary education institutions as a proportion of total expenditure on all educational institutions (2003) Public and private institutions	25.2	24.8	13/29	102
Total public expenditure on tertiary education (2003) Direct public expenditure on tertiary institutions plus public subsidies to households (which include subsidies for living costs, and other private entities)				
As a percentage of total public expenditure[18]	-	3.1	-	-
As a percentage of GDP	1.3	1.3	11/29	100
Subsidies for financial aid to students as a percentage of total public expenditure on tertiary education (2003)				
Scholarships / other grants to households	12.1	9.8	14/28	123
Student loans	13.7	7.1	8/17	193
Scholarships / other grants to households attributable for educational institutions	1.4	1.6	7/10	88
Expenditure on institutions by service category as a percentage of GDP (2003)				
Educational core services	0.78	1.06	21/25	74
Ancillary services (transport, meals, housing provided by institutions)	-	0.06	-	-
Research and development	0.48	0.38	6/25	126

	Netherlands	OECD mean	Netherlands' rank[1]	% to OECD mean[2]
Expenditure on tertiary education institutions by resource category (2003) Distribution of total and current expenditure on tertiary education institutions from public and private sources Percentage of total expenditure				
Current	95.2	89.7	5/27	106
Capital	4.8	10.3	23/27	47
Percentage of current expenditure				
Compensation of teachers	-	43.0	-	-
Compensation of other staff	-	23.4	-	-
Compensation of all staff	74.6	65.5	7/28	114
Other current	25.4	34.5	22/28	74
Registration and tuition fees (2002/03)[19] Source: Eurydice (2005) Registration and tuition fees and other payments made by students of full-time undergraduate courses, public sector				
Neither fees nor compulsory contributions		9/35	-	-
Solely contributions to student organisations		3/35	-	-
Registration and/or tuition fees (and possible contributions to student organisations)	√	23/35	-	-

LITERACY LEVELS

	Netherlands	OECD mean	Netherlands' rank[1]	% to OECD mean[2]
IALS achievement levels of graduates aged 25-34 (1994-1995) Source: IALS				
Graduates aged 25-34 at IALS levels 1 and 2 as a per cent of total graduates aged 25-34	10	19	16/21	53
Graduates aged 25-34 at IALS levels 4 and 5 as a per cent of total graduates aged 25-34	48	40	7/21	120

	Netherlands	OECD mean	Netherlands' rank[1]	% to OECD mean[2]
PATTERNS of PROVISION				
Ratio of students to teaching staff in tertiary education[20] (2004) Based on full-time equivalents, Public and private institutions.				
Type B	-	15.9	-	-
Type A and advanced research programmes	-	16.3	-	-
Tertiary education all	13.6	15.5	13/24	88
EXPECTATIONS OF 15-YEAR-OLD STUDENTS				
Students' expected educational levels (2003) Source: PISA 2003 (OECD, 2004) Per cent of 15-year-old students who expect to complete secondary education, general programmes (ISCED 3A)	40.0	48.9	21/28	82
Per cent of 15-year-old students who expect to complete secondary education, vocational programmes (ISCED 3B or C)	-	29.9	-	-
Per cent of 15-year-old students who expect to complete post-secondary non-tertiary education (ISCED 4)	24.9	16.4	3/21	152
Per cent of 15-year-old students who expect to complete tertiary-type B education (ISCED 5B)	-	20.5	-	-
Per cent of 15-year-old students who expect to complete tertiary-type A education or an advanced research qualification (ISCED 5A or 6)	40.6	44.0	16/29	92
RESEARCH AND DEVELOPMENT				
Gross domestic expenditure on Research and Development (R&D) as a percentage of GDP Source: OECD (2006)				
2004	1.78	2.25	12/26	79
1995	1.97	2.07	9/27	95

	Netherlands	OECD mean	Netherlands' rank[1]	% to OECD mean[2]
Higher education[21] expenditure on R&D as a percentage of GDP Source: OECD (2006)				
2004	0.50	0.39	6/26	128
1995	0.57	0.34	3/27	168
Percentage of gross domestic expenditure on R&D by sector of performance (2004) Source: OECD (2006)				
higher education	27.9	17.3	9/26	161
(higher education in 1995)	28.8	16.3	7/26	177
business enterprise	57.8	68.0	18/26	85
government	14.4	12.1	11/20	119
private non-profit sector	0	2.6	-	-
Percentage of higher education expenditure on R&D financed by industry Source: OECD (2006)				
2003	6.8	6.0	8/24	113
1995	4.0	6.2	19/27	65
Total researchers per thousand total employment Source: OECD (2006)				
2003	4.5	-	15/22	-
1995	4.9	5.8	12/25	84
Researchers as a percentage of national total (full time equivalent) (2003) Source: OECD (2006)				
higher education	27.4	-	-	136
(higher education in 1995)	36.6	26.9	13/26	-
business enterprise	51.7	-	-	-
government	20.6	-	-	-
Share in OECD total "triadic" patent families[22] (%) Source: OECD (2006)				
2003	1.97	-	6/30	-
1997	1.96	-	7/30	-
Foreign PhD students as a per cent of total PhD enrolments (2003)	-	13.7	-	-

Notes for the Tables

Sources:

All data are from Education at a Glance, OECD Indicators 2004, 2005 and 2006, unless indicated otherwise in the table.

Other sources:

Eurydice (2005), *Key data on education in Europe 2005*, Eurydice, Brussels

IALS, *International adult literacy survey database*

OECD (2004), *Learning for Tomorrow's World, First Results from PISA 2003*, OECD, Paris

OECD (2006), *Main Science and Technology Indicators, volume 2006/2*, OECD, Paris

General notes:

1. "NTL's rank" indicates the position of NTL when countries are ranked in descending order from the highest to lowest value on the indicator concerned. For example, on the first indicator *"% of the population aged 25-64 with tertiary qualifications, Tertiary-type B - Total"*, the rank *"x/x"* indicates that NTL recorded the xx[st] highest value of the xx OECD countries that reported relevant data. The symbol "=" means that at least one other country has the same rank.

2. "% to OECD mean" indicates NTL's value as a per cent of the OECD value. For example, on the first indicator *"% of the population aged 25-64 with tertiary qualifications, Tertiary-type B - Total"*, the percentage *"xx"* indicates that NTL's value is equivalent to xx% of the OECD mean.

3. The calculation of the average years in formal education is based upon the weighted theoretical duration of schooling to achieve a given level of education, according to the current duration of educational programmes as reported in the UOE data collection.

4. Two alternative methods were employed to calculate the average duration of tertiary studies: the approximation formula and the chain method. For both methods, it should be noted that the result does not give the average duration needed for a student to graduate since all students participating in tertiary education are taken into account, including drop-outs. Hence, the figure can be interpreted as the average length of time for which students stay in tertiary education until they either graduate or drop out.

5. This indicators show the ratio of graduates as a proportion to all fields of studies. The fields of education used follow the revised ISCED classification by field of education.

6. The employed are defined as those who during the survey reference week: *i)* work for pay (employees) or profit (self-employed and unpaid family workers) for at least one hour, or *ii)* have a job but are temporarily not at work (through injury, illness, holiday, strike or lockout, educational or training leave, maternity or parental leave, etc.) and have a formal attachment to their job.

7. The unemployed are defined as individuals who are without work, actively seeking employment and currently available to start work.

8. The impact of demographic change on total enrolment is calculated by applying the enrolment rates measured in 1995 to the population data for 2003: population change was taken into account while enrolment rates by single year of age were kept constant at the 1995 level.

9. The impact of changing enrolment rates is calculated by applying the enrolment rates measured in 2003 to the population data for 1995: the enrolment rates by single year of age for 2003 are multiplied by the population by single year of age for 1995 to obtain the total number of students that could be expected if the population had been constant since 1995.

10. The net entry rates represent the proportion of persons of a synthetic age cohort who enter a certain level of tertiary education at one point during their lives.

11. Educational institutions are classified as either *public* or *private* according to whether a public agency or a private entity has the ultimate power to make decisions concerning the institution's affairs. An institution is classified as *private* if it is controlled and managed by a non-governmental organisation (*e.g.,* a Church, a Trade Union or a business enterprise), or if its Governing Board consists mostly of members not selected by a public agency. The terms *"government-dependent"* and *"independent"* refer only to the degree of a private institution's dependence on funding from government sources. A *government-dependent private institution* is one that receives more than 50% of its core funding from government agencies. An *independent private institution* is one that receives less than 50% of its core funding from government agencies.

12. Students are classified as foreign students if they are not citizens of the country for which the data are collected. Countries unable to provide data or estimates for non-nationals on the basis of their passports were requested to substitute data according to a related alternative criterion, *e.g.,* the country of residence, the non-national mother tongue or non-national parentage.

13. The number of students studying abroad is obtained from the report of the countries of destination. Students studying in countries which did not report to the OECD are not included in this indicator.

14. This indicator covers residents in the country, regardless of citizenship and of educational or labour market status.

15. School expectancy (in years) under current conditions excludes all education for children younger than five years. It includes adult persons of all ages who are enrolled in formal education. School expectancy is calculated by adding the net enrolment rates for each single year of age.

16. In this indicator, the column "OECD mean" indicates the number of Eurydice member countries/areas, in which limitation on admission to tertiary education is adopted, out of 35 countries/areas whose data is available. For example, in the column "Limitation at national level with direct control of selection", 1/35 indicates that limitation at national level with direct control of selection is adopted in 1 country.

17. The estimates of cumulative expenditure on education over the average duration of tertiary studies were obtained by multiplying annual expenditure per student by an estimate of the average duration of tertiary studies.

OECD REVIEWS OF TERTIARY EDUCATION – NETHERLANDS – ISBN 978-92-64-03925-4 – © OECD 2008

18. Total public expenditure on all services, excluding education, includes expenditure on debt servicing (*e.g.* interest payments) that are not included in public expenditure on education.

19. "Registration fees" refers to payments related to registration itself or the certified assessment of each student. By "tuition fees" is meant contributions to the cost of education supported by individual tertiary education institutions. These fees also include any certification fees. Payments for entrance examinations are excluded. In this indicator, the column "OECD mean" indicates the number of Eurydice member countries/areas, in which registration and tuition fees are adopted, out of 35 countries/areas whose data is available. For example, in the column "Membership fees to student organisations", 5/35 indicates that membership fees are adopted in 5 countries/areas.

20. "Teaching staff" refers to professional personnel directly involved in teaching students.

21. "Higher Education" includes all universities, colleges of technology and other institutions of post-secondary education, whatever their source of finance or legal status. It also includes all research institutes, experimental stations and clinics operating under the direct control of or administered by or associated with higher education institutions. For detail, see OECD (2002), *Frascati Manual 2002: Proposed Standard Practice for Surveys on Research and Experimental Development.*

22. "Triadic patent" means patents filed all together to the European Patent Office (EPO), the US Patent and Trademark Office (USPTO) and the Japanese Patent Office (JPO). This indicator shows each country's share in total triadic patents filed by OECD countries. Reference year is when the priority patent is filed. Data is estimated by the OECD Secretariat and provisional. Because a few countries share large proportion of triadic patents, other countries have small share.

Country specific notes:

[i.] Due to discrepant data, averages have not been calculated individually.

[ii.] Only tertiary type A.

OECD PUBLICATIONS, 2, rue André-Pascal, 75775 PARIS CEDEX 16
PRINTED IN FRANCE
(91 2008 15 1 P) ISBN 978-92-64-03925-4 – No. 56447 2008

CPSIA information can be obtained at www.ICGtesting.com
Printed in the USA
244054LV00002B/3/P

9 789264 039254